Australian Encounters

Australian Encounters
Australian Encounters

Cornelsen

Australian Encounters

Herausgegeben von
Dr. Bernd Klewitz, Kirchhain-Schönbach

Verlagsredaktion
Marc Proulx, Bettina Schaschke (Assistenz)

Umschlaggestaltung
Knut Waisznor

Layout und technische Umsetzung
Gisela Hoffmann

www.cornelsen.de

1. Auflage, 4. Druck 2008 / 06

Alle Drucke dieser Auflage sind inhaltlich unverändert
und können im Unterricht nebeneinander verwendet werden.

Druck: CS-Druck Cornelsen Stürtz, Berlin

ISBN 978-3-464-06829-8

Inhalt gedruckt auf säurefreiem Papier aus nachhaltiger Forstwirtschaft.

Contents

Abbreviations and symbols

abbr	abbreviation
adj	adjective
adv	adverb
AE	mainly or exclusively American English
AustE	mainly or exclusively Australian English
BE	mainly or exclusively British English
cf.	Lat. *confer* = compare; see
derog	derogatory
e.g.	Lat. *exempli gratia* = for example
esp.	especially
etc.	Lat. *et cetera* = and so on
fig	figurative
fml	formal
i.e.	Lat. *id est* = that is
infml	informal
l., ll.	line, lines
n	noun
p., pp.	page, pages
pl	plural
prep	preposition
sb.	somebody
sing	singular
sl	slang
sth.	something
U	uncountable noun
usu.	usually
v	verb
vulg	vulgar

Where two pronunciations of a word are given in the annotations, the first is the standard British English, the second (after the symbol ☆) the standard American English pronunciation. Regular differences in American pronunciation from the British – as for instance the [-r] after vowels – have not been given.

The pronunciation of English in Australia is generally similar to BE rather than AE.

Perspectives on Life and the Land

1 Waltzing Matilda A.B. 'Banjo' Paterson

For many outsiders, Australia brings to mind images of koalas, kangaroos and Ayers Rock. For most Australians, however, the song 'Waltzing Matilda', which was written in 1895, is still the most loved national icon. The folk song is so popular that a movement in the 1970s almost succeeded in making it the country's national anthem.

Oh, there once was a swagman camped in the billabong,
Under the shade of a coolabah tree,
And he sang as he looked at the old billy boiling,
'Who'll come a-waltzing Matilda with me?'

Chorus:
Who'll come a-waltzing Matilda, my darling,
Who'll come a-waltzing Matilda with me?
Waltzing Matilda and leading a waterbag
Who'll come a-waltzing Matilda with me?

Down came the jumbuck to drink at the waterhole,
Up jumped the swagman and grabbed him with glee,
And he sang as he put him away in his tucker-bag,
'You'll come a-waltzing Matilda with me.'

Swagmen carrying their swags and billys in 'Sundowners' (1881)

Who'll come a-waltzing Matilda, my darling,
Who'll come a-waltzing Matilda with me?
Waltzing Matilda and leading a waterbag,
Who'll come a-waltzing Matilda with me?

Up came the squatter a-riding his thoroughbred,
Up came policemen – one, two, and three,
'Whose is that jumbuck you've got in the tucker-bag?
You'll come a-waltzing Matilda with me.'

Who'll come a-waltzing Matilda, my darling,
Who'll come a-waltzing Matilda with me?
Waltzing Matilda and leading a waterbag,
Who'll come a-waltzing Matilda with me?

The swagman he up and he jumped in the waterhole,
Drowning himself by the coolabah tree,
And his ghost may be heard as it sings by the billabong,
'Who'll come a-waltzing Matilda with me?'

Who'll come a-waltzing Matilda, my darling,
Who'll come a-waltzing Matilda with me?
Waltzing Matilda and leading a waterbag,
Who'll come a-waltzing Matilda with me?

1 *swagman* (AustE): travelling labourer who carries all his belongings rolled up in a blanket or cloth called a swag **1** *billabong* (AustE): Aboriginal name for a pool of deep water **2** *Coolabah* (AustE): Aboriginal name for a eucalyptus or gum tree **3** *billy:* metal can or pot for boiling water, etc., over a campfire **4** *waltzing Matilda* (AustE sl): walking a long distance while carrying a swag (see *swagman*, l. 1) **10** *jumbuck* (AustE): sheep **11** *with glee:* happily **12** *tucker-bag* (AustE infml): bag used for carrying food **18** *squatter:* (in Australia) wealthy land owner; farmer of sheep or cattle on a large scale **18** *thoroughbred* ['θʌrəbred]: horse of high quality that has parents that are both of the same breed

1. Describe the main characters and their roles in the story.
2. Who do you think the swagman is addressing when he says 'my darling' (l. 6)?
3. How is the chorus different from the rest of the lyrics in the song?
4. In your view, what is the meaning behind the swagman's death?
5. Many Australians feel that 'Waltzing Matilda' should be the country's national anthem. Why do you think this simple song about a swagman is so popular in Australia?

2 Waltzing the Outback Geoffrey Blainey

Social historian Geoffrey Blainey has written about what he calls the 'tyranny of distance' faced by those living on the vast, thinly populated Australian continent. In this feature article for the Melbourne newspaper *The Age*, Blainey describes how people's perception of the Australian outback has changed over the course of history and what this means for urban Australians today.

The outback is central to how Australians see themselves and their country. But most have never been outback: huge numbers don't even look out the aircraft window to inspect the outback from on high.

Of course nobody fully knows the outback. It is too huge, too varied, for one person to know. But it is packaged for our consumption in slogans and paintings, poems and TV; and so nearly every Australian has some picture of it.

That picture of the outback has changed drastically in the past; and it will probably change again in the coming century.

'Outback' was originally two separate words. In perhaps the earliest printed reference, The *Wagga Wagga Advertiser* of 17 April 1869 reported that drovers were taking sheep through the town, for the grass 'will be abundant out back' following the recent rain. Outback remained as two words even in 1896 when Henry Lawson published his book *While the Billy Boils*. But he showed a change was coming, for he coupled the words 'out-back' together with a hyphen.

In those days the cities viewed the outback with some hope, for it might hold pockets of riches. They also feared it. Exploring parties, led by Leichhardt and Burke and Wills had met disaster there. In the outback fights and acts of violence between black and white were frequent. The few geography books written for Australian schools warned of the dangers of the outback where even the overland telegraph stations were built like little forts, in case 'the blacks become numerous and troublesome'.

The outback was deemed difficult but it was never dismissed. Much of it was viewed strategically as important. Australians believed the future of the outback, especially the tropical outback, would be profoundly affected for better or worse by what happened in nearby nations. Curiously, that belief has faded though it has also been muted somewhat by the vogue for political correctness.

In Melbourne and Sydney the outback was once feared as the source of the clouds of dust that descended during summer storms. Towns like Oodnadatta and Burketown were seen as unlivable. For several decades the people who lived in most outback regions had to pay a high life insurance surcharge because the outback was seen as risky to health, and the tropical outback was a special risk.

At the same time the Heidelberg painters were helping to make the outback seem more familiar, even though they painted far from the outback. Lawson's short stories helped to make the 'Back of Bourke' feel more habitable to people living in Melbourne and Sydney. Lawson was fascinated by outback people but he disliked the outback. The endless plains, the stunted bush often gave him the creeps. 'The least horrible spot in the bush,' he once wrote, was where 'a green crop is trying to grow' in a

place once covered by native vegetation. He sometimes remarked that the scenery in the outback was funereal or like a dreary ocean.

Waltzing Matilda reflects that ambivalent feeling. Today it is seen instinctively as an outback song, and relished as such, but it could not have become popular if it had caught the essence of the outback. If 'Banjo' Paterson had placed his swagman near Ayers Rock the song would have been neglected. Instead the setting for his swagman is decidedly friendly with its expanse of water, its shade and its choice fresh meat. Except for the coolabah tree, the swagman could have been boiling his billy by a billabong within sight of the Melbourne-Sydney road.

Slowly the attitude to the outback was changing. Cities like Broken Hill and Kalgoorlie – and they were counted among Australia's 12 largest cities in 1900 – appeared in what had been viewed as the outback. Railways pushed some way into the interior. A string of isolated ports such as Derby and Normanton became gateways to the Never Never; and often their bush hospitals nursed outback people.

Aircraft cut the isolation of parts of the outback. Qantas began its life in western Queensland, carrying a few passengers and mailbags from town to town. In August 1927 the Royal Flying Doctor Service was born when Dr George Simpson hired a little Qantas plane so an injured miner could be flown from the new Mt Isa field to the hospital across the ranges at Cloncurry.

Cities and near-coastal towns held the bulk of the population, and they largely shaped Australian attitudes. Cities were now more sympathetic to the Australian environment and the outback, largely through the work of painters and writers. The outback was the most distinctive part of the continent, and nationalists usually choose what is distinctive as a symbol of their nation. The qualities that distinguished many outback people – mateship, courage, determination – were increasingly seen, rightly or wrongly, as part of that vague concept, the national character.

By the 1980s the outback no longer seemed hostile in the eyes of city Australians. It could be visited with ease and safety on a flying holiday. It was being tamed by jet aircraft, air conditioning, the mobile phone, the 4-wheel drive. It was also tamed by television and the new breed of documentary in which Aborigines and Nature, once both seen as threatening, were depicted as friendly. In one of the remarkable changes of Australian history the word wilderness, once seen as perturbing, became benign.

Ayers Rock symbolised the profound change. In 1900 nobody would have dreamed of making the Rock a symbol of Australia. In 1940 its ranking as a national symbol was well below the small statue of Gundagai's Dog on the Tuckerbox. And yet now, under its new name of Uluru, it is one of Australia's three best known landmarks. Heavy advertising and tourist boosting have accentuated this change but public opinion is sympathetic.

Maybe the swing in city attitudes toward the outback is permanent but probably it is not. The outback will never be viewed with neutral eyes. It will be a mirror of Australian attitudes to Nature, to Aborigines, economic development, mines and reservoirs, and even attitudes to Asia. It will continue to be a mirror of how Australia's people and cities see themselves.

A medic of the Royal Flying Doctor Service treats an emergency patient on location.

8 *consumption:* act of using food, energy, resources, etc.; (here, fig) use **17** *drover:* person who drives animal herds over long distances
18 *abundant* [ə'bʌndənt]: more than enough **21** *billy:* metal can or pot for boiling water, etc., over a camp fire **23** *couple sth. with sth.:* combine sth. with sth. **24** *hyphen* ['haɪfn]: Bindestrich **33–34** *overland telegraph station:* (in Australia) pole connecting telegraph lines in the bush or outback **36** *deem sth.* (fml): consider or regard sth. **37** *dismiss sth.:* put sth. (usu. thoughts, feelings, etc.) out of one's mind **40–41** *for better or worse:* so oder so **42** *fade:* lose or make sth. lose strength, colour or freshness **43** *mute sth.:* not express sth. openly or strongly • *vogue* [vəʊg]: fashion; (here) trend **47** *descend* [dɪ'send]: come or go down **51** *life insurance:* Lebensversicherung • *surcharge:* extra payment **54** *Heidelberg painters:* group of Australian painters during the 1880s and 1890s who painted scenes of the bush; named after the suburb of Melbourne where most of them lived **58** *habitable* ['hæbɪtəbl]: fit to live in **62** *stunted* (adj): stopped from growing or developing to full size • *give sb. the creeps:* make sb. afraid and cause an unpleasant sensation in their skin **64** *crop:* plant that is grown in large quantities **65** *native* (adj): particular to a region **67** *funereal* [fju'nɪəriəl]: suitable for a funeral (= Beerdigung); miserable • *dreary:* dull, gloomy **70** *relish sth.:* enjoy or get pleasure from sth. **73** *swagman* (AustE): travelling labourer who carries all his belongings rolled up in a blanket or cloth called a swag • *Ayers Rock* ['eəz]: world's largest monolith, located in the Northern Territory of Australia, also called Uluru **74** *neglect sth.:* give no or not enough care or attention to sth. **77** *coolabah* (AustE): Aboriginal name for the eucalyptus or gum tree **78** *billabong* (AustE): Aboriginal name for a pool of deep water **87** *Never Never:* (in Australia) remote desert country, as in western Queensland or Central Australia **90** *Qantas* (abbr) = *Queensland and National Territory Aerial Service:* Australian national airline
91 *mailbag:* large sack for carrying letters, etc.
96 *range:* line or row of mountains, hills, etc. **97** *the bulk of:* the majority of **106** *distinguish sb./sth.:* make sb./sth. different • *mateship* (AustE): comradeship of friends, usu. male, viewed as an institution **107** *determination:* quality of being firmly committed to doing sth. **111** *hostile* ['hɒstaɪl ☆ 'hɑːstl]: of or relating to an enemy; unfriendly **103** *tame sth.:* make sth. easy to control, no longer wild **115** *breed:* type, sort **116** *Aborigine* [ˌæbə'rɪdʒəni]: inhabitant of a place, esp. Australia, from a very early period **118** *depict sth.:* describe sth. in words **119–120** *wilderness* ['wɪld-]: area that is not cultivated or settled **120** *perturbing* (fml) (adj): worrying or disturbing • *benign* [bɪ'naɪn]: kind, gentle, pleasant **124** *ranking* (n): position on a scale **125–126** *Gundagai's Dog on the Tuckerbox:* reference to a 19th century bush ballad in which a settler's dog 'sat on the tuckerbox five miles from Gundagai' and refused to help its master **127–128** *landmark:* object that is easily seen and recognized from a distance **128** *boosting* (n): increasing the numbers of sth. **131** *swing* (n): change

1. According to Blainey, how well do Australians know their outback?
2. By the middle of the 19th century people in the cities had mixed feelings about the outback. Find examples in the text that illustrate these differing attitudes.

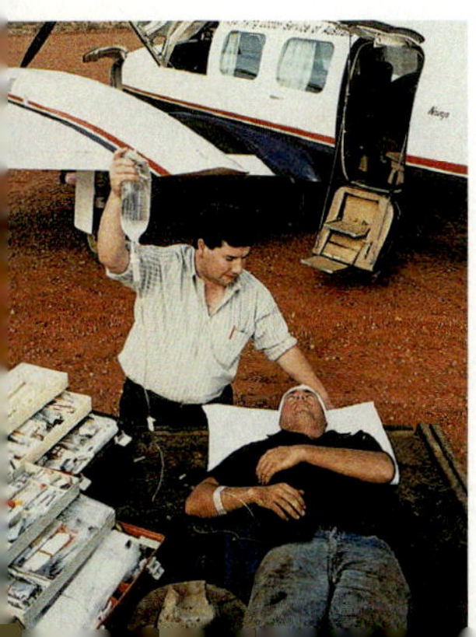

3. What events influenced the change in people's attitude towards the outback?
4. Based on what you know about the song 'Waltzing Matilda' (cf. Text 1), how would you interpret the title of Blainey's article? What do you think the writer means?
5. Comment on Blainey's statement in the first and last sentence of the article.
6. What does the term 'outback' suggest when you think of Australia today?

Australia – An Overview

Geography and climate

Lying between the Indian and Pacific Oceans, Australia has an area of 7,682,300 sq km (roughly the size of the 48 mainland states of the USA). The continent stretches about 4000 km from east to west and 3200 km from north to south. Topographically Australia can be divided into three major areas: the Eastern Highlands, the Central Lowlands and the Western Plateau. The vast central area, known as the 'outback', is mostly flat desert with some low mountains, including the mysterious Uluru (Ayers Rock) and Kata Tjuta (the Olgas) as well as the beautiful MacDonnell Ranges near Alice Springs. The extreme north of Australia, also known as the Top End, is a tropical region. In the lower half of the continent fertile areas are limited to a few narrow strips along the east and south coasts.

The climate is relatively harsh and dry in large parts of the continent, more moderate in the south and east, and tropical in the north. As the Australian seasons are the opposite of those in Europe, many Australians spend Christmas on the beach, and winter begins in June. The two biggest cities, Sydney and Melbourne, enjoy moderate climates with winter temperatures rarely reaching freezing point and warm sunny days in the summer.

*Population, rural and urban areas**

Australia has roughly 20 million inhabitants, 77% of whom are Australian-born and 23% coming from other countries. The population is concentrated mainly along the east coast in the states of New South Wales (6.5 million), Victoria (4.9 million) and Queensland (3.9 million) and in the southern coastal region of Western Australia (1.9 million). Relatively few people live in the dry centre of the continent. Australia's indigenous population, the Aborigines and Torres Strait Islanders, number about 430,000 and live mostly in central Australia or in the far north. Most Australians (more than 85%) live in urban centres. Sydney (4 million) and Melbourne (3.6 million) are the country's two main urban areas.

Administration and politics

The Commonwealth of Australia consists of six states and two territories: New South Wales, Victoria, Tasmania, Southern Australia, Western Australia, Queensland, the Northern Territory and the Australian Capital Territory (ACT). Canberra, the country's capital, is – like Washington, DC, the capital of the USA – located in its own separate administrative area (the ACT).

Australia has a parliamentary system of government, with a federal government (run by the prime minister and his cabinet) and individual state governments. The federal government is elected every three years. Voting is compulsory for everyone who is 18 years of age or older. The federal parliament

* *Statistics from 2007, Australian Bureau of Statistics*

Melbourne (above); Parliament House, Canberra (below)

consists of two houses: the House of Representatives (lower house) and the Senate (upper house). The main political parties are the Australian Labor Party, the Liberal Party and the National Party. The Liberal and National parties traditionally make up a coalition. Although Australia is still a monarchy with the British monarch as its head of state, the country enjoys full autonomy. The British sovereign is represented by the governor-general and the state governors. In 1999 a national referendum calling for a republic was defeated by a clear majority.

Industry

Australia is an affluent, industrialised nation with its wealth stemming largely from agriculture and mining. Agriculture today accounts for about 4% of production, while mining contributes around 8% and manufacturing roughly 16%. Major commodity exports include wool (Australia is the world's largest supplier), wheat, barley, sugar, coal and iron ore. Tourism is also an important source of income.

Environmental issues and conservation

Australia's unique and varied natural environment includes tropical rainforests and wetlands in the north, offshore coral reefs in the east, eucalyptus forests in the southeast and desert lands in the centre. This environment has been under increasing threat since the first Europeans arrived on the continent in the 18th century. The land was occupied by farmers and ranchers who were unfamiliar with the continent's regional conditions and its delicate balance of plant and animal life. The overgrazing of cattle and sheep caused further destruction. As a result, in New South Wales alone, areas the size of England are virtually wasteland today.

Sheep station, Western Australia (above); Great Barrier Reef, Queensland (right)

Already by the late 1800s conservationists were working to protect the environment. More recently, organizations such as Greenpeace, Friends of the Earth and the Wilderness Society have been active in raising public awareness, influencing government policy and battling big business interests that threaten the environment. Through the activities of such groups numerous environmentally sensitive areas – the Great Barrier Reef, the Tasmanian Wilderness and the Wet Tropics, to name a few – have been preserved. Today there are more than 500 national parks and protected wilderness areas.

3 To Honour Nature

Marlo Morgan

The novel *Mutant Message Down Under* (1991) by US author Marlo Morgan tells of a white woman's experience on 'walkabout' with Australian Aborigines. A US doctor goes to Australia to work on an inner-city project for young Aborigines. When the indigenous community invites her to experience their way of life, she does not know that this will involve a hard four-month trek through the red desert. Here she describes part of this journey and the people who gradually change her view of life.

I was awakened in the morning before any exposure to sun rays by the noise from people gathering up the few scattered articles we had used the evening before. I was told the days gained in heat, so we would walk during the cooler morning hours, rest, and then resume our journey into the later night. I folded the dingo hide and handed it to a man who was packing. The hides were left easily accessible, because during the peak heat of the day, we would find shelter, build a *wiltja*, or temporary brush shelter, or use our sleeping skins to construct shade.

Most of the animals do not like the glaring sun. Only the lizards, spiders and bush flies are alert and active at one hundred plus degrees. Even snakes must bury themselves in the extreme heat, or they become dehydrated and die. It is hard sometimes to spot snakes as they hear us coming and peek their heads out of the sandy soil to find the source of the vibration. I am grateful

People of Arnhem Land, Northern Territory, at sunset; a man repairing tools for hunting (right); a woman hunting rabbits (below)

that at the time I was not aware there are two hundred different types of snakes in Australia, and more than seventy are poisonous.

I did learn that day, however, the remarkable relationship the Aborigines have with nature. Before we started walking for the day, we formed a close-knit semicircle, all of us facing the east. The Tribal Elder moved to the center and started chanting. A beat was established and carried through by each person clapping their hands, stomping their feet, or hitting their thighs. It lasted about fifteen minutes. This was routine each morning, and I discovered that it was a very important part of our life together. It was morning (prayer, centering, goal setting, whatever you want to call it). These people believe everything exists on the planet for a reason. Everything has a purpose. There are no freaks, misfits, or accidents. There are only misunderstandings and mysteries not yet revealed to mortal man.

The purpose of the plant kingdom is to feed animals and humans, to hold the soil together, to enhance beauty, to balance the atmosphere. I was told the plants and trees sing to us humans silently, and all they ask in return is for us to sing to them. My scientific mind immediately translated this to mean nature's oxygen-carbon dioxide exchange. The primary purpose of the animal is not to feed humans, but it agrees to that when necessary. It is to balance the atmosphere, and be a companion and teacher by example. So each morning the tribe sends out a thought or message to the animals and plants in front of us. They say, 'We are walking your way. We are coming to honor your purpose for existence.' It is up to the plants and animals to make their own arrangements about who will be chosen.

The Real People tribe never go without food. Always, the universe responds to their mind-talk. They believe the world is a place of abundance. Just as you and I might gather to listen to someone play the piano, and honor that talent and purpose, they sincerely do the same thing with everything in nature. When a snake appeared on our path, it was obviously there to provide our dinner. The daily food was a very important part of our evening celebration. I learned that the appearance of food was not taken for granted. It was first requested, always expected to appear, and did appear, but was gratefully received and genuine gratitude was always given. The tribe begins each day by saying thank you to Oneness for the day, for themselves, their friends, and the world. They sometimes ask for specifics, but it is always phrased 'If it is my highest good and the highest good for all life everywhere'.

After the morning semicircle gathering, I tried to tell Ooota it was time for him to take me back to the jeep, but it seemed he was nowhere in sight. Finally, I acknowledged I could endure one more day.

The tribe carried no provisions. They planted no crops; they participated in no harvest. They walked the blazing Australian Outback, knowing each day they would receive bountiful blessings of the universe. The universe never disappointed them.

We ate no breakfast the first day, and I found that to be the usual pattern. Sometimes our meal was at night; however, we ate whenever the food appeared, regardless of the position of the sun. Many times we ate a bite here and there, not a meal as we know it.

We carried several bladder water vessels. I know that humans are approximately 70 percent water and require a minimum of one gallon per day under ideal conditions. Observing the Aborigines, I saw they did require much less, and drank less than I. In fact, they rarely drank from the water containers. Their bodies seemed to use the moisture in food to a maximum. They believe Mutants have many addictions, and water is included.

We used the water to soak what appeared to be dead and dried-out weeds at mealtime. The brown stubs went into the water as lifeless, dehydrated sticks and came out many times miraculously looking like fresh celery stalks. They could find water where there was absolutely no appearance of moisture. Sometimes they would lie down on the sand and hear water underneath or hold their hands with the palm down and scan the ground for water. They put long hollow reeds into the earth, sucked on the end, and created a minifountain. The water was sandy and a dark color but tasted pure and refreshing. They were aware of water in the distance by watching the heat vapors and could even smell and feel it in the breeze. I now understand why so many people who try to explore the inner regions die so quickly. It would take the native expertise to survive.

1–2 *exposure to sth.:* state of being in a place or situation without protection from sth. harmful or unpleasant **3** *scattered* (adj): spread about **7** *hide:* animal's skin **15** *spot sb./sth.:* see or notice sb./sth., esp. suddenly or when it is not easy to do **19** *poisonous:* giftig *honour* (BE) = (AE) honor sb./sth.: show great respect for sb./sth. **22–23** *close-knit* (adj): (of a group of people) strongly united by shared beliefs, interests, acitivities, etc.; (here) gathered closely together **24** *chant* (v): sing or shout sth. repeatedly, using the same rhythm **25** *stomp* (infml): move, walk, dance, etc. with a heavy step **26** *thigh* [θaɪ]: part of the human leg between the hip and the knee **30** *freak:* person who is considered abnormal because of their behaviour, appearance or ideas; very unusual and unexpected event or action **31** *mortal:* sterblich **33** *enhance sth.:* improve sth. **36** *oxygen-carbon dioxide:* Sauerstoff-Kohlendioxid **43** *Real People:* (in the novel) name taken by the Aboriginal tribe **44** *abundance* [əˈbʌndəns]: quantity that is more than enough **49** *take sth. for granted:* think of sth. as being guaranteed **57** *acknowledge sth.:* accept the truth of sth.; admit sth. **58** *provisions* (pl): Verpflegung, Proviant • *crop:* plant that is grown in large quantities **59** *harvest* (n): act of cutting and gathering food crops (cf. *crop*, l. 58) **60** *harvest* (n): act of cutting and gathering food crops (cf. *crop*, l. 58)

A circle of tribal elders

64 *blessing* (n): sth. that is good or helpful **66** *bladder water vessel:* container for carrying water and made from an animal's bladder (= Blase) **67** *approximate* [əˈprɒksɪmət ☆ -ˈprɑːk-]: similar in quality, amount, etc., but not exactly the same **70** *moisture:* wetness **71** *Mutant* [ˈmjuːtənt]: living thing with an abnormal or frightening appearance as a result of genetic change; (in the novel) name given to white people by the Aboriginal tribe **73** *stub:* small piece of sth. remaining after it has been shortened through use **74** *stalk:* Stange **77** *palm* [pɑːm]: inner surface of the hand between the wrist (= Handgelenk) and fingers • *scan sth.:* examine sth. with great attention

1. According to the author, what beliefs do the Aboriginal people hold concerning life on this planet and the role of plants and animals (cf. ll. 29–54)?
2. Why does the tribe not carry any food during their walkabout?
3. Describe how the people in the text find and make use of the scarce water resources in the desert.
4. Find three examples of how the 'Real People' see or do things differently from our typical Western view or approach. Explain the differences.
5. The Aboriginal tribe in the novel call themselves 'Real People' (l. 43) and refer to people in our civilization as 'Mutants' (l. 71). Why do you think this is and how does this reflect their world view?

4 Australia A. D. Hope

A.D. Hope (1907–2000), the son of a Presbyterian minister, grew up in rural New South Wales and Tasmania (see the map, inside cover). After finishing school in Sydney he accepted a scholarship to Oxford. He returned to Australia in 1931 and tried various occupations before becoming lecturer and later professor of English at Australian National University. Hope won numerous national and international awards for his poetry. The poem 'Australia' was first published in his *Collected Poems* (1972).

A Nation of trees, drab green and desolate grey
In the field uniform of modern wars,
Darkens her hills, those endless, outstretched paws
Of Sphinx demolished or stone lion worn away.

They call her a young country, but they lie:
She is the last of lands, the emptiest,
A woman beyond her change of life, a breast
Still tender but within the womb is dry.

Without songs, architecture, history:
The emotions and superstitions of younger lands,
Her rivers of water drown among inland sands,
The river of her immense stupidity

Floods her monotonous tribes from Cairns to Perth.
In them at last the ultimate men arrive
Whose boast is not: 'we live' but 'we survive',
A type who will inhabit the dying earth.

And her five cities, like five teeming sores,
Each drains her: a vast parasite robber-state
Where second-hand Europeans pullulate
Timidly on the edge of alien shores.

Yet there are some like me turn gladly home
From the lush jungle of modern thought, to find
The Arabian desert of the human mind,
Hoping, if still from the deserts the prophets come,

Such savage and scarlet as no green hills dare
Springs in that waste, some spirit which escapes
The learned doubt, the chatter of cultured apes
Which is called civilization over there.

1 *drab* (adj): dull, not interesting • *desolate* ['desələt] (adj): (of a place) empty and lifeless 3 *paw:* foot of a four-legged animal with claws (= Krallen) 4 *Sphinx:* monster from Greek mythology with a woman's head and a lion's body, noted for killing those who could not answer its riddle • *wear sth. away – wore – worn:* damage sth. by wear or use 8 *tender* (adj): delicate, easily damaged or hurt • *womb* [wu:m]: female organ in which the baby or young is carried while it develops before birth 10 *superstition:* Aberglaube 15 *boast* (n): statement showing too much pride and satisfaction 17 *teeming* (adj): present in great numbers • *sore:* wunde Stelle 18 *parasite* (usu. *parasitic*) (adj): always relying on or making use of others and giving nothing in return 19 *pullulate* ['pʌljuleɪt] (v): (of animals, etc.) breed rapidly or in large numbers 20 *alien* ['eɪliən]: foreign, strange 22 *lush* [lʌʃ]: plentiful 25 *scarlet:* bright red or reddish orange 27 *chatter* (n): continuous rapid talk

1. Describe how the speaker in the poem views Australia's trees and hills. What do they represent?
2. According to the speaker, why is it a 'lie' (l. 5) to call Australia a young country?
3. From the speaker's point of view, what does Australia lack and what is the reason for the country's 'immense stupidity' (l. 12)?
4. How are Australia's major cities and their inhabitants characterised?
5. Hope's poem is full of symbolism. Find and explain three examples of metaphor.
6. How do the last two stanzas differ from the rest of the poem? What sentiment does the speaker express in lines 21–28?
7. Get together with a partner or in small groups and discuss and make notes on the author's attitude toward Australia. Compare your conclusions with those of other groups.

From the Beginning: A History

Early Aboriginals in Western Australia, ca. 40,000 BC

Long before Europeans arrived, the Australian continent was home to Aboriginal peoples. Archaeological evidence suggests that Aborigines were already living in Australia over 40,000 years ago. In pre-European times they lived in small groups as hunters, fishers and gatherers, roaming over large areas of land. There were an estimated 300,000 Aborigines living on the Australian continent and in Tasmania by the time of the first white settlements. They were killed in large numbers by settlers and by diseases introduced by the Europeans.

Although the English captain James Cook is usually credited with having discovered Australia in 1770, the Dutch explorer Willem Jansz was probably the first European to set eyes on the country in 1606. Only months later the Spaniard Luis Vaez de Torres sailed the north coast, giving the Torres Strait its name.

In 1770 Captain James Cook charted the east coast and claimed it for Britain, as no other European country had taken formal possession. After the loss of its American colonies, Britain began looking for another place to send its convicted criminals and thus, in 1788 the first British penal colony was established at Port Jackson (now Sydney). Free settlers had already begun migrating to Australia in the 1770s. The transportation of convicts gradually lost support in both Australia and Britain and the system was stopped in 1840. Altogether, around 160,000 convicts were sent to Australia. In the same period roughly 409,000 free settlers arrived on the continent.

In 1850 Britain granted self-government to the Australian colonies, but the independent nature of the colonies created a number of problems, e.g. they developed different railway gauges and postal systems, and had no common defence policy. Talks on a federation began and were completed on January 1,

Captain James Cook and his party land at Botany Bay (Sydney), April 28, 1770

1901, when the colonies of New South Wales, Victoria, Queensland, South Australia, Western Australia and Tasmania formed the Commonwealth of Australia (the Northern Territory joined in 1911). In 1911 Canberra became the capital and the Australian Capital Territory (ACT) was formed. The federal government of Australia was given control of foreign affairs, defence, trade, etc., with a governor-general as representative of the head of state, appointed by the British monarch.

In one of its first official acts in 1901, the federal government introduced the so-called 'White Australia Policy', which restricted non-white immigration. The new policy was particularly directed against Chinese immigrants who worked in the gold fields since the first gold rush in 1851 and Pacific Islanders who worked as labourers in the north. This policy was maintained up until 1972.

Australian soldiers head off to war in Europe, 1940 (left).

Aboriginal activist Donna Gibbs in Canberra, 2000 (below)

During both World Wars (and again in later regional conflicts) Australia sent troops to fight alongside the British. Following the end of World War II the country became a destination for large numbers of war refugees from Europe.

Indigenous Australians, who were previously denied many rights, finally won the right to vote in 1967 and for the first time received access to social benefits. This marked the beginning of a new government policy to end discrimination and impoverishment of the indigenous peoples. While the new policy gave Aborigines equal rights, they still faced an uphill struggle to improve their situation. Aboriginal activism began to gather force. In 1972, in a symbolic protest that drew much attention, Aborigines occupied the lawn outside Parliament House in Canberra, setting up a tent which they called the Aboriginal or Tent Embassy. Today Aboriginal activists continue to alert the Australian public to the critical situation of the indigenous population.

As Britain's political and economic interests and attention have gradually shifted towards Europe in recent decades, Australia's governments have worked to strengthen political and economic ties with their Asian neighbours.

5 On Having Half a Ball Ross Campbell

Ross Campbell (1910–1982), a former Rhodes scholar to Oxford, was educated at Melbourne University and worked as a journalist in Sydney up until the Second World War, during which he served in the Royal Australian Air Force. In several books published later he continued in the tradition of a long line of ironic Australian humorists. In this essay he points out Australia's place in the world – which, he insists, is not necessarily at the bottom.

The largest English-speaking city in the Southern Hemisphere! This boast is made about Sydney in a travel folder. It sounds impressive enough till you remember that most of the big English-speaking cities are in the Northern Hemisphere.

It is the same when someone brags of having the biggest hat factory or the most valuable stamp collection in the Southern Hemisphere. The other hat factories and stamp collections south of the equator do not offer first-class competition. The biggest ones are probably in Brazil – but who knows or cares what they have in Brazil?

Mind you, I don't want to run down the Southern Hemisphere. I was born there, and have resided there for most of my life. A man has a natural sense of loyalty to his home hemisphere. I believe ours is as big as any other hemisphere in the world. It is an old-established one, and has an assured future. Yet, fond as we are of the old hemisphere, we should not blind ourselves to its shortcomings.

Chief of these is that so much of it is water. The Pacific Ocean, especially, is bigger than we could wish. When the land masses were handed out, the Northern Hemisphere got more than its fair share. That is one reason for its attitude of superiority.

Our hemisphere has another handicap – the late start it made in the progress business. The native inhabitants, such as the Australian Aborigines and the Bantus, were decent but conservative folk. The hemisphere did not go ahead until visitors from the North moved in. This has encouraged Northerners to treat the Southern Hemisphere as a country branch office. They gave it contemptuous names like 'the Antipodes' and 'the flip side of the world'.

I would like to do some plain speaking about the Northern Hemisphere. It has admirable features, but it is too stuck-up. Granted, it contains the biggest hat factories, the most valuable stamp collections, etc. These advantages are largely the result of the Northern Hemisphere's luck in getting in first.

Among other things, it had the advantage of drawing the first maps. It put the Northern Hemisphere on top, and ours at the bottom. That is why we have to put up with being referred to patronisingly as 'down under'.

There is no reason, apart from custom, why the Southern Hemisphere should not be on top and London and New York 'down under'. An organisation should perhaps be founded to manufacture maps and globes of this upside-down kind. It would remind Northerners that they have no geographic right to consider themselves top people. The organisation could be called Friends of the Southern Hemisphere.

You notice one sign of their self-confidence north of the Equator – they don't restrict their boasting. Nobody declares a hat factory (or atomic pile, or Christmas pudding) to be the biggest in the Northern Hemisphere. They call it the biggest in the world. It is taken for granted that the hillbillies of the Southern Hemisphere have nothing like it.

How feeble, by contrast, is the Australian habit of claiming that something is the biggest in the Southern Hemisphere. It suffers from the weakness of qualified superlatives. It is like saying that So-and-so is the greatest mathematician in Woy Woy; or that Mrs C. is the best-dressed woman in Broome.

I suggest that we give up hemispherical boasting. We impress nobody by going the half hog. We only remind them that many things really are bigger in the Northern Hemisphere.

The Southern Hemisphere is still a good place for the average family. I have been to the Northern Hemisphere, so I know what I'm talking about. It's all right for a holiday, but you wouldn't want to live there.

Not that I hold with hemisphere prejudice. It is out of place in the democratic world of today. A man should be judged on his merits, not asked what hemisphere he comes from. After all, we all belong to the same sphere.

I would go further and say that any boasting about things being the biggest or best should be avoided. As a journalist I have found that if you say Mrs C. is the best-dressed woman in Broome, some nuisance is sure to write to the editor: 'Mrs. D. is well known to be the best-dressed woman in Broome.' It is safer, as well as more modest, not to say your hat factory is the biggest in the Southern Hemisphere. Just say you have a big hat factory (assuming that you do have one).

have a ball (infml): have fun **2** *boast* (n): statement showing too much pride and satisfaction **7** *brag:* talk with too much pride about sth. **15** *run sb./sth. down* (infml): talk about sb./sth. in a negative way, criticize sb./sth. **17** *reside* [rɪ'zaɪd]: have one's home in a certain place **21** *assured* [ə'ʃʊəd] (adj): guaranteed **23** *shortcoming* (n) (pl): weakness • *decent* ['diːsənt]: proper, respectable **33** *Bantu:* member of any of the indigenous Negroid peoples of southern, eastern and central Africa **37–38** *country branch office:* small and unimportant office of a large company located in a remote area **38** *contemptuous:* feeling or showing that sb./sth. is not important and does not deserve respect **38–39** *the Antipodes* [æn'tɪpəˌdiːz]: Australia and New Zealand, so named by the British because the two countries are situated opposite Greenwich, England, on the earth's surface **39** *flip side:* reverse side **42** *stuck-up* (infml) (derog): having a proud, superior attitude towards others • *granted* (adv): used to show that you accept that sth. is true, often before you make another statement about it **51** *patronising* (adj): gönnerhaft, herablassend **62** *restrict:* limit **67** *hillbilly* (infml) (derog): person from a remote hilly or mountainous area **69** *feeble* (derog): lacking force, not effective **74** *Woy Woy:* small inland Australian town, 45 km north of Sydney **75** *Broome:* remote town and holiday resort in Western Australia **77–78** *go the half hog* (infml): not do sth. to the full extent **86** *prejudice* ['predʒudɪs]: irrational dislike or distrust of a person, group, custom, etc. **89** *merit* (pl): fact, action or quality that is good and deserves praise **98** *nuisance* ['njuːsns ☆ nuː-] (n): sb./sth. that is annoying or causes trouble **102** *modest* ['mɒdɪst ☆ mɑː-]: not talking proudly about your abilities or achievements

1. In Campbell's view, what is wrong with the claim that Sydney is 'The largest English-speaking city in the Southern Hemisphere' (ll. 1–2)?

2. What 'shortcomings' (l. 23) does the writer point out about the southern hemisphere?

3. According to the text, what terms have people in the northern hemisphere typically used to refer to the southern part of the globe? Why does Campbell find these terms 'contemptuous' (l. 38) and 'patronising' (l. 51)?

4. Describe the tone of the text. Give examples to support your conclusion.

5. How does the writer make fun of the practice of making comparisons between North and South? Give examples.

6. Based on your own knowledge, to what extent are attitudes in the North towards countries in the southern hemisphere a serious concern?

The Australian Dream

1 The Story of Djangkawu Terry Gandadila

To Australia's Aboriginal people, the land and all living things were created in the 'Dreamtime', a creation time in the spiritual realm. Dreamtime stories, or 'songs', which have been preserved and passed on for thousands of years, tell about the interaction between the spirits and nature. They also communicate a group's history, laws, customs and rituals. This is a Dreamtime story from the Murrungun/ Djinang people of Arnhem Land in Australia's Northern Territory. It is told by Terry Gandadila, a Murrungun artist and writer.

The story tells of Djangkawu, the spirit creator in the spirit world *(Burralku)* who had two eggs. He made the world with one egg, but it was bad. He cracked the second egg and it was good. Djangkawu and his daughters, the Djangkawa sisters, and his son, Mambu, sent a messenger to earth to see if everything was alright. His name was Malawurrwurr *(Mukarr)*. He wore the arm bands of a messenger and he carried a spear and a woomera. He came to earth, at a time of flood, through the Bulawirri waterhole on the island of Galiwin'ku (Elcho Island). Here he made a stringy-bark canoe *(derrka)* and, following the western star, he travelled from Galiwin'ku across the Arafura Sea. He tried to spear a long-tom fish *(larrdjidja)* but it was too big to be pulled into the canoe. He collected seaweed *(wunuwun)* from the shores of the Miwirnbi flood plains and wove a rope to tie up his canoe. There he saw pelicans *(nanydja)* and this told him that the land was drying up, becoming hard, and that the flood was over.

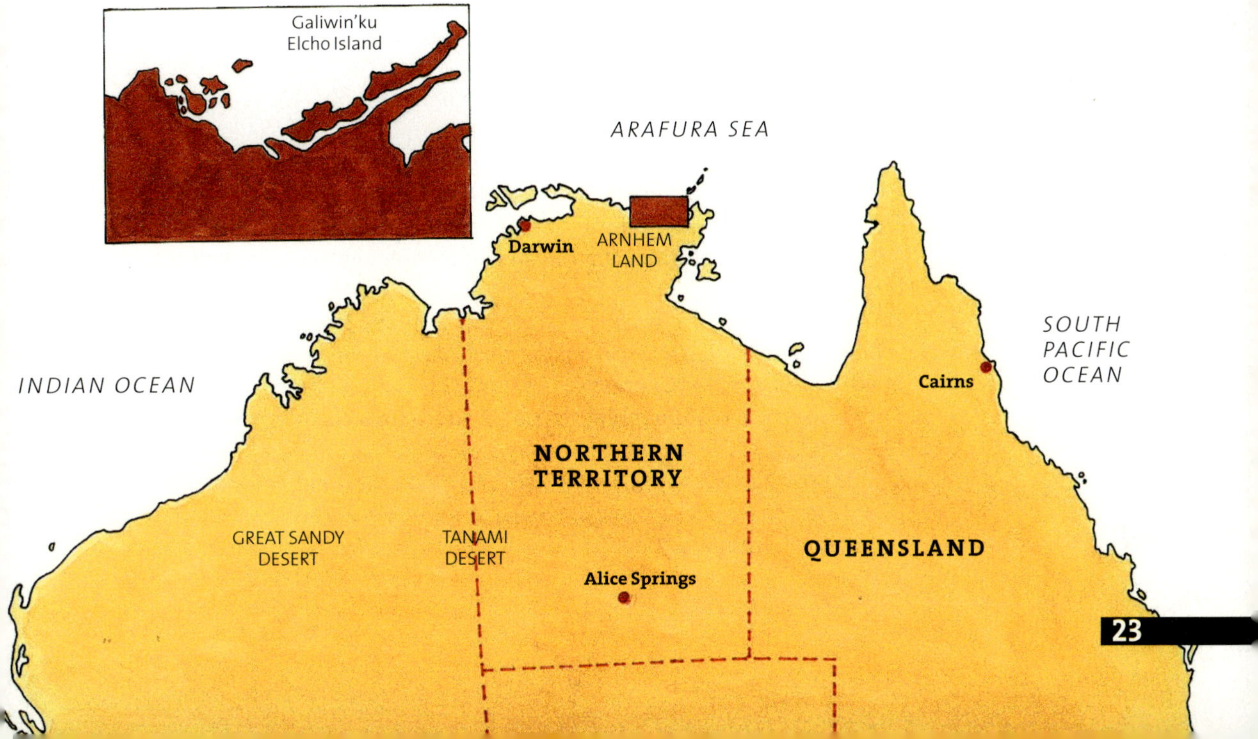

The full moon brings King tides and the Miwirnbi flood plains get covered with plenty of fish. Here Mukarr caught and ate a butterfish *(murrpini)*. He found some swamp grass *(gunumbirri)* and roasted the roots over the fire and ate them (they taste like peanuts). He heard the sound of brolgas *(gururrki)* and this told him there was a waterhole nearby – he followed the sound to the waterhole. He named it Bulawirri because it had the same familiar feeling as the Bulawirri waterhole on the island of Galiwin'ku. Travelling on, over the flood plains he saw three women. He named them Gurdidi, Garrala and Berreperrepe. [...] These women were from his same moiety, Duwa *(djowung)*, but he still chose to marry them. This is not permitted by law. They each bore him a son. The son of his youngest wife was special and Mukarr named him Ran.gu. After the boys were born, Mukarr's wives were transformed into birds, because he had broken the law. Then the wet season wind *(mardawurr)* came telling him it was time to move on.

Mukarr began his return to Galiwin'ku. When the wind started to blow he sailed in his canoe from the Miwirnbi flood plains and came to the island of Djimarlu. This island was different, it was all green. Here Mukarr noticed the leaves of the yam *(barrtji)* had changed colour. He knew this was a sign to light a bushfire *(duwarr)* in order to clear the land for new growth. So he lit a bushfire by rubbing two sticks together. The fire covered the whole island and also accidentally the neighbouring island of Milingimbi. Mukarr walked through the land and left his footprints in the ash. He found a goanna *(djarrka)* which he cooked and ate. In the rainforest Mukarr saw the butterflies *(bunpa)* dancing and he knew the monsoon rains were coming soon. The dragonfly *(migiwirrwarr)* danced to tell him that it was time to harvest fish and yam. When he found the banyan tree *(djanpa)* he ate the fruit *(ginydja)* then collected the bark and made a string bag.

The Munyal Spirits live in the rainforest. Here the idea came to him to make a Morning Star Pole *(marradjiri)*. He saw the spear tree *(wardawarda)* and he thought the tree would make a good pole. He found vines *(barday)* and knew they were good for making arm bands. He made the Morning Star Pole with the two feather tassels, one to the west representing the evening star, and one to the east representing the morning star. The feather tassels were made of lorikeet and ibis feathers. Djangdjang are the long strings. When the Munyal spirits saw Mukarr making the Morning Star Pole they were very excited because he had made a symbol of the spirit of Barnumbirr. Encouraged, the Munyal Spirits whispered to him how to dance and how to sing for each living thing. Mukarr listened to their instructions, they came to him as ideas.

He heard the owls in the night. Their call sounded like a didgeridoo, so he named them *Djurdutjurdu*. From the bush carrot *(marrpanda)* leaves, which are sticky when they are crushed, he made the glue for the Morning Star Pole. The carrots he collected for his journey back to Galiwin'ku. The dance of the Morning Star came to him in this way.

Mukarr dug up some cheeky potatoes *(yukurda)* and cooked some for dinner. In the morning he saw the wallabies *(ngarrku)* and speared and ate one of them. He saw a glider possum *(warpurr)* go into its house in the hollow

trunk of a tree *(gorrtje)*. This was a sign to Mukarr that this hollow stringy-bark tree was easy to make into a canoe and that it was time for him to return to the spirit world to give his report to Djangkawu, Mambu, and the Djangkawa sisters. He sang a special song to give thanks to the glider possum. Then he left the island and returned to the spirit world and gave his report that everything on the earth was good. Djangkawu sent him back to the island of Galiwin'ku.

On the island of Galiwin'ku he saw how the ants *(giyany)*, in making a new nest, had dug out some red ochre. Spirits told him how the columns of ants travelling into the nest were just like the people travelling from the north, south, east and west to the special island of Djimarlu. He took the red ochre

'Barnumbirr Manikay II' (1988), by Jack Wunuwun, from the Morning Star Cycle, which tells the story of Mukarr's journey.

and put it in a specially made dillybag to bring to the Bulawirri waterhole. Here he told the people there that the red ochre would now show who belongs to the Duwa *(djowung)* clan group. The waterhole picture shows Mukarr's journeys, his footprints travel to north, south, east and west. The centre circle represents the island of Djimarlu. Mukarr had broken the law by taking wives from his own clan group so Mambu punished Mukarr by setting fire to his house *(humpy)* with a bolt of lightning. Mukarr transformed himself into a crow and flew up into a tree to avoid being burnt. Mambu later showed forgiveness and transformed Mukarr into a man. At the same time, his son Ran.gu became the moon, the Djangkawa sisters had to face each other and became the sun, and Mambu became the Morning Star. Mukarr was banished from the Murrungun clan group and joined the Marrangu clan. He was assigned the task of always bearing witness to the Morning Star. Today, when the people of Miwirnbi and Galiwin'ku come together to perform the Morning Star Ceremony, Marrangu clan group elders are always present as witnesses.

3 *crack sth.:* break sth. open or into pieces **4** *messenger* [-dʒə]: person who carries messages **6** *woomera* (AustE): wooden stick with a hook, used by Aboriginal peoples of Australia for throwing a spear or dart **8** *stringy-bark:* of the bark (= Rinde) of a eucalyptus tree **18** *brolga* (AustE): large grey Australian crane (= Kranich) **24** *moiety* ['mɔɪəti] (n): one of two groups within a tribe, both of which are formed on the basis of descent (= Abstammung) **32** *yam:* Yamswurzel **36** *goanna* (AustE) [gəʊ'ænə]: any of various Australian monitor lizards **38** *monsoon:* seasonal wind of South Asia that brings heavy rainfall **46** *tassel:* bunch of threads tied at one end and hanging free at the other, used as a decoration **48** *lorikeet:* Australasian parrot **51** *whisper:* speak softly
54 *didgeridoo* (AustE) [ˌdɪdʒəri'du:]: deep-toned Aboriginal musical wind instrument, made of a section of bamboo or other hollow wood **56** *glue:* Klebstoff
60 *wallaby:* Australian animal like a small kangaroo **61** *glider possum:* australische Art Beutelratte, die zwischen Bäume springt **62** *trunk:* main woody base of a tree **70** *ochre* ['əʊkə]: type of red or yellow earth used as pigment for paints and dyes **73** *dillybag* (AustE): small bag used for carrying food or water **79** *bolt of lightning:* Blitzstrahl **84** *banish sb. (from sth.):* send sb. away, esp. out of a country, as a punishment **85** *assign sth. to sb.:* give sth. to sb. as their share of work or responsibility • *bear witness to sth.:* be present to see or observe sth.

Above:
'Malawurrwurr'
(ancestor/messenger),
1988, Jack Wunuwun

Right:
'Derrka'
(stringy-bark canoe),
1988, Jack Wunuwun

1. Which of the events in the story could be called acts of 'creation' and which were acts of 'consumption'? Make two lists and connect those acts which are directly related to each other.
2. Explain in your own words how Mukarr's journey helped create a certain ceremony that is practiced today (cf. ll. 42–58, 77–88).
3. Analyse and discuss the way the spirits interact with the earthly world through their messenger in this story.
4. What importance might this particular story have for the people of Miwirnbi and Galiwin'ku? Use examples from the story.
5. Find a story or song from your country or another traditional culture (e.g. Native American) whose purpose is similar to that of the Aboriginal Dreamtime songs. Share your findings in class.
6. Compare and contrast the ways in which religious beliefs shape people's attitudes in Western society and in Aboriginal culture. Consider, for instance, differing ideas about creation and humans' relationship to nature (see also Ch. I, Text 3).

'Larrdjidja' (long-tom fish), 1988, Jack Wunuwun

(All paintings are from The Holmes à Court Collection, Heytesbury.)

2 The Future of Multiculturalism

Kerry-Anne Walsh

Meeting the needs of an ever-changing multi-ethnic population has become one of Australia's greatest challenges. In the area of education this challenge is particularly visible. In the following excerpt from an article in the magazine *The Bulletin*, Kerry-Anne Walsh looks at one high school and its important role in the country's 'multicultural experiment'.

It is 9 am and hundreds of children have swarmed through the gates of Marrickville High, a crowded, boisterous school in the inner west of cosmopolitan Sydney. 'My children' is how headmaster Andy Powell proudly describes the throng of 760 students who crowd the campus, hidden among the terraced houses and light industrial factories.

This is no ordinary school, but is the future face of Australia: 92% of Powell's charges come from non-English-speaking backgrounds. Those whose family's native language is English make up only 7.4%. Sixty teachers from 10 ethnic backgrounds guide the children through an ever-more diverse education curriculum that attempts to embrace the needs of multicultural schooling.

Marrickville was the early settling ground of Italian, Greek and Yugoslav settlers who came to Australia in the first wave of immigration after World War II. They took factory and menial jobs, congregated in the low-rent district and eventually brought out their extended families to join them. They have been there ever since, spreading to the surrounding suburbs as they became more affluent until the inner west took on an identity of its own as the multicultural hub of Sydney.

Now their numbers have been swelled by the late 1970s and '80s wave of migrants: Indochinese, Arab, Portuguese and Chinese among others. Powell's roll book tells the story not only of this school, but of the impact of diverse migration on Australia's now less-dominant

Anglo-Celtic society. Main cultural groups at the school, in order of numbers, are Greek, Vietnamese, Arabic, Portuguese, English-speaking, Chinese and Pacific Islander. Other backgrounds include Macedonian, Turkish, Indian, Filipino, Italian and Indonesian.

Interpreters: Parents' newsletters are translated into four main languages. Separate parents' meetings are held in the languages of their birth and conducted through translators. Telephone interpreters are often used if parents need to be contacted during the day. While Powell stresses that many parents can converse in English, he says they feel more comfortable using their native tongue when discussing complex curriculum and educational issues.

Four languages are taught as part of the curriculum and evening and weekend classes are held in eight or nine different languages. This satisfies strong parental desires for children to retain their heritage and gives students an extra subject for more marks. Powell believes there is a strong appreciation of the educational opportunities available in Australia. Many of his students have classes six days a week and at nights.

So what does being Australian mean to this future generation – Australia's managers of the next century? 'They all feel very much Australian, but also very much part of their own cultures,' says Powell. 'Those that have been born here perhaps feel more Australian than their parents. That perhaps creates a bit of a problem for them, not for us.

'Most of them are quite proud, and we encourage them to be proud, of their cultural background. We don't encourage them to think of themselves as English Australians; we encourage them to think of themselves as Arabic-speaking Australians or Greek-speaking Australians or whatever, and to value their heritage.' Powell says that any problems the children may have are not due to their ethnic backgrounds, but their socio-economic situations.

Values: A group of students expands on how they feel about living in Australia, their values and the values of their parents, some of whom arrived with the first wave of migrants and who still have not adopted the language and customs of their new country. All agree that their parents tend to associate only with members of their own communities, but this younger generation is mixing more freely. However, because of where they live, that does not include many Anglo-Australians.

Rita, born here, says of her Greek-born parents: 'They still strongly identify themselves with Greece and they try to keep the customs. In my case I try to identify myself with the Greek culture but it's really hard to just have that one [culture]. I consider myself an Australian with a Greek background.'

Maria from Indonesia: 'My parents want me to keep my tradition and I want to mix with Australians, too, so I have to learn what is acceptable. Sometimes it's hard. If I talk to Australians, they want you to be open but with my own people you hide your feelings. Sometimes you have to think what to say.'

Australia's population by birthplace*

(Major countries of birth over a 20-year period)

Country of birth	**1981**	**1991**	**2001**
Australia	11,388.8	13,318.8	14,931.2
UK and Ireland	1120.9	1244.3	1182.8
New Zealand	160.7	286.4	394.1
Italy	275.0	272.0	238.5
Vietnam	40.7	124.8	169.5
China**	25.2	84.6	157.0
Greece	145.8	147.4	132.5
Germany	109.3	120.4	117.5
Philippines	14.8	79.1	112.2
India	41.0	66.2	103.6
Netherlands	95.1	100.9	91.2
Other	1099.6	1439.2	1783.2
Total overseas	3128.1	3965.3	4482.1
Total	**14,516.9**	**17,284.1**	**19,413.3**

* in thousands

**excluding SARs (Hong Kong, Macau) & Taiwan Province

Source: Australian Bureau of Statistics

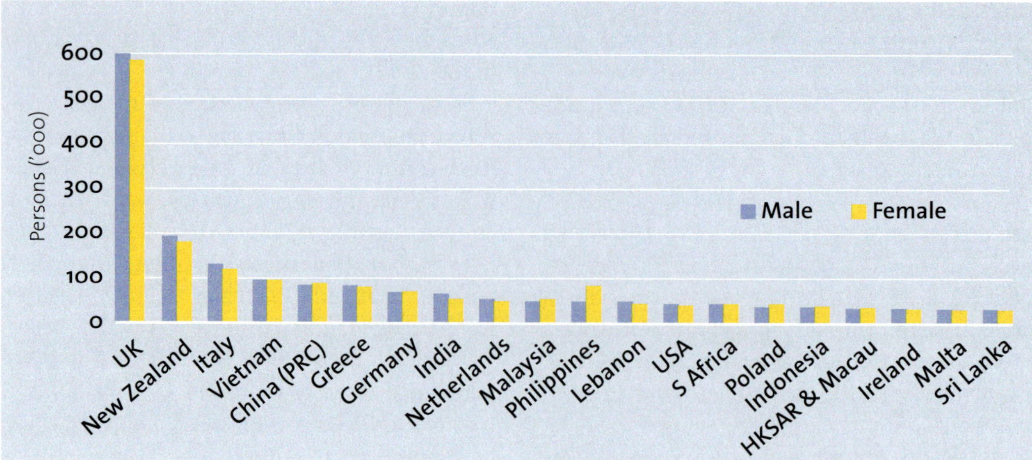

Numbers of overseas born – by birthplace and sex
Source: Australian Bureau of Statistics, 1999

Amanda, born here, says of her Lebanese parents: 'Their memories are at home, they think about things that remind them about their home country. But they look at Australia as a place with better opportunities for them and us.' She says they mix only with the Lebanese community.

3 *boisterous:* loud, noisy **6** *throng* (n): large group of people **15** *diverse:* very different from each other and of various kinds **16** *embrace sth.* (fml): include sth. **21** *menial* ['mi:niəl] (adj): not skilled or important, and often boring or badly paid **26** *affluent* ['- - -]: prosperous or rich **28** *hub* (n): central and most important part of a place or activity **29** *swell:* increase in size or volume **32** *roll book:* list containing the names of students **55** *retain sth.* (fml): keep sth.; continue to have sth. • *heritage* (sing): history, traditions and qualities which define the character of a country or society **78** *socio-economic:* involving both social and economic factors **79** *expand on sth.:* speak or write at length or in detail about sth.

1. Why is Marrickville High in Sydney 'no ordinary school' (l. 9)? How does the school reflect the area of Marrickville?

2. How does Marrickville High serve the language needs and desires of both parents and students?

3. Describe in your own words the school's teaching philosophy with regards to students of different cultural backgrounds.

4. How does Walsh get the reader's attention at the beginning of her article? What other stylistic and structural techniques does the writer use to make her article more interesting?

5. Look at the table on p. 29. What general historic trends can you conclude from the statistics given here? How does this information compare with the main cultural groups at Marrickville High (cf. ll. 35–38)?

6. Discuss your own school's approach to teaching students of different cultural backgrounds. What do you find good or bad about this approach?

7. To what extent is language important for a person's identity? Explain and discuss.

A Land of Immigrants

Early migration

The first migrants were the Aborigines themselves, who arrived on the continent tens of thousands of years ago, most likely from neighbouring Asian regions to the north.

From the arrival of the first British settlers in 1788 up to 1850, Australia's population gradually increased as Britain transported convicts to its eastern colonies. The first group of eleven free immigrants arrived in Sydney in 1793. By 1830 only about 14,000 free immigrants had settled in Australia. Over the next 20 years assisted immigration by colonial governments increased the numbers to almost half a million. Gold mining then changed the pattern of growth dramatically: between 1850 and 1860 the population of all the colonies almost tripled from 405,400 to 1,145,600.

A changing population

When the colonies became a federation in 1901 a new immigration policy was adopted. The Immigration Restriction Act, known as the White Australia Policy, was designed to prevent Asians and Pacific Islanders from settling there. Prospective immigrants had to pass a dictation test in a European language. This language could be as obscure as the authorities wished. The test was also used to keep out immigrants unwanted for political reasons. The German-Czech writer Egon Erwin Kisch, trying to enter Australia in 1934, was given a test in Gaelic. He failed, of course, and forced his entry by jumping from a ship in Melbourne and breaking his leg. The dictation test was not abolished until 1958.

Until the Second World War Australians were mainly of English, Scottish and Irish descent. But just before the outbreak of the war several thousand Jewish refugees who had been forced out of Germany and other German-occupied countries in Europe arrived in Australia. Military invasion became a real fear, and it was believed that the country could only be safe in future if a lot more people lived there. 'Populate or perish' became the slogan. A new immigration scheme was introduced.

European immigrant families arriving in Sydney, 1948

In the immediate post-war years Australia became involved in the resettlement of refugees from eastern Europe. The influx of 171,000 eastern Europeans marked a significant change in Australia's approach of giving preference to settlers from the UK, who before 1947 were the only settlers who received government assistance. The government entered into formal agreements to sponsor migration from a number of European countries, including Germany, the Netherlands, Italy, Greece and Malta. Southern European migration further broadened the origins of Australia's migrants, although the majority of these people received no government assistance and had to rely on relatives.

In another major policy change, in the 1950s and 1960s small numbers of non-Europeans were admitted if they could show skills and qualifications that were needed in Australia.

A new era

The last major phase of Australian migration began in the 1970s, when the Whitlam government (Labor) abandoned the White Australia Policy. Discrimination on the grounds of race, colour or nationality was no longer allowed in the selection of immigrants. This new policy signalled a change in social attitudes, but was also a response to the loss of Australia's principal trading partner when Britain joined the European Common Market in 1973.

In the late 1980s and early 1990s changing economic circumstances led the government to heavily restrict migrant their immigrant quotas. Since then Australia has taken on large influxes of Asians, particularly political and economic refugees from Vietnam. On the whole, these 'New Australians' have been remarkably well accepted. More recently, the government has been confronted with increasing numbers of refugees, mainly from Middle Eastern countries, who have arrived in Australia illegally by boat. The question of how to deal with these asylum seekers is a hot political issue in Australia (see this chapter, Text 3).

Asian refugees in an immigration centre, 1995

In 2005, 23.7 per cent of Australians had been born overseas – much the same proportion as in the year of Federation, 1901.

Australia's overseas-born population (in thousands)	
United Kingdom	1137.4
New Zealand	455.1
Italy	224.3
China	191.2
Vietnam	177.7
India	138.7
Philippines	129.4
Greece	127.2
Germany	115.2
South Africa	113.8
Malaysia	100.3
Netherlands	87.7
Lebanon	85.3
Hong Kong (SAR of China)	76.2
Other countries	1670.0
Total overseas-born	**4829.5**
Total population	20,328.6

Source: Australian Bureau of Statistics, 2005

3 A Cry for Freedom and a Better Life

In July 2000 illegal immigrants broke out of an immigration detention centre in the South Australian town of Woomera to protest the poor, prison-like conditions there. International attention suddenly focused on the government's controversial handling of illegal immigrants, many of whom are political and economic refugees. The Melbourne newspaper *The Age* of July 7, 2000, commented on the government's dilemma of balancing effective immigration control with the proper treatment of people seeking asylum.

Below left and center: Asian and Middle Eastern refugees at Woomera Detention Centre

The Government believes it is important not to encourage refugees to enter the country by boat. It argues that, not only is such a course dangerous for the refugees themselves, these unannounced arrivals by sea have forced greater spending on coastal surveillance and accommodation for detainees. The Government estimates that the cost of intercepting, detaining and processing illegal arrivals could rise to $1 billion over the next four years if the trends continue. The trouble is that the trends are determined by factors well outside Australia's control: the people-smuggling racket is run by criminal gangs, and the asylum seekers, for the most part, are escaping from countries in Asia, Africa and the Middle East. Some have been tortured, some are seeking political asylum. The steady increase in the number of people arriving illegally by boat suggests that, regardless of the Federal Government's wishes to the contrary, the impulse to seek freedom and a better life cannot easily be snuffed out. Although we may prefer our asylum seekers to use more formal channels, we have a moral duty to treat uninvited visitors with justice and compassion. And it is on these grounds that the detainees may have legitimate grounds for complaint.

Unfortunately, mean-spiritedness has characterised Australia's refugee policy in recent years. Many were dismayed at the Government's decision to repatriate those Kosovar refugees who wanted to stay. Before last week's breakout at Woomera, there had been strikes and incidences of violence at the camp. In April, two men escaped from the detention centre amid a protest involving some of the camp's 1300 inhabitants. The men were later found at Port Augusta. The incident prompted Amnesty International to call for an end to the mandatory detention of illegal immigrants. The human rights organisation has argued that, as well as being more humane, it would be cheaper to keep refugees in community centres.

Boat people are not the only illegal immigrants in Australia. But they are the most publicised, and they get the harshest reception. Most of the estimated 53,000 illegal immigrants in the country arrived by air and overstayed their visas. They are tourists, students or people granted temporary-residence permits. They do not get much media attention and the Government does not appear to consider them a serious threat. Those Woomera refugees who are released will do it hard. They will be given $500 and a three-year temporary-protection visa. Although most of them do not speak English, they will not be eligible for some of the Commonwealth support services to which other refugees are entitled, such as language and job-search assistance. South Australia's Premier John Olsen has described the temporary-visa policy as harsh and inconsistent. The same could be said of mandatory detention. A more generous and compassionate approach might have prevented the detention centre breakouts.

6 *surveillance* [sɜːˈveɪləns]: act of carefully watching a person suspected of a crime or a place where a crime may be committed **7** *detainee* (n): person who is kept in a prison or other official place and prevented from leaving **8** *intercept sb./sth.:* stop or catch sb./sth. that is going from one place to another • *detain sb.:* keep sb. in an official place (e.g. a police station, prison or hospital) and prevent them from leaving **13** *racket* (infml): dishonest or illegal way of getting money **17** *torture sb.* [ˈtɔːtʃə]: jn. foltern **22** *snuff sth. out:* stop or destroy sth. completely **25** *compassion:* strong feeling of sympathy for people who are suffering and a desire to help them **30** *dismay sb.:* make sb. feel shocked and disappointed **31** *repatriate sb.* [-ˈpæt- ☆ -ˈpeɪt-]: send or bring sb. back to their own country • *Kosovar* (adj): of or from Kosovo, an autonomous region in south-western Serbia **37–38** *Port Augusta:* town in the Australian state of South Australia (cf. the map, inside cover) **38** *prompt sb. to do sth.:* make sb. decide to do sth. **39** *mandatory* (fml): required by law **46** *harsh:* treating people in a very cruel or strict way **57** *eligible for sth.* [ˈelɪdʒəbl]: able to have sth. because you have the right qualifications, are old enough, etc. **58** *Commonwealth:* official name used to refer to Australia **62** *inconsistent:* widersprüchlich, unbeständig; inkonsequent

1. According to the text, why does the Australian government want to discourage refugees from entering the country by boat?

2. Why, in the view of the writer, are Australian authorities unable to control the influx of refugees?

3. What exactly is the writer's position regarding refugees? Explain, using examples from the text.

4. Write a letter to the editor of *The Age* explaining why you agree or disagree with the opinion in the commentary. Share your letter with the class.

5. Working in pairs or groups, collect further up-to-date information from the Internet and other sources on illegal immigration in Australia. Then find out about the situation in your own country. Put together a final comparison and present your results to the class.

6. Organize a classroom debate on the Australian government's handling of the refugee problem. One group should represent the government's position, while the other group can represent Amnesty International or another human rights group. Prepare your arguments beforehand, gathering information from other sources if necessary.

Residents of Narre Warren, 'a place of space, safety and stability'

4 A Home on the Edge

Sally Heath, Mark Baker

In a land of wide open spaces, many young Australians still realize their dream of having a house of their own. In one of a series of articles in 1998 on changing patterns of settlement within Australia, a Melbourne newspaper looked at life on the expanding outward edges of the city. Here is an excerpt.

The city of Casey is a fertile place. Grasslands are lush. Housing estates run across the hills like mountain rivers. And babies are as commonplace as rooftiles. Each week about 35 families move to the municipality on Melbourne's eastern fringe – inching out from their childhood suburbs to secure a similar lifestyle for their own children. A place of space, safety and stability.

Ask a handful of people who have moved to Narre Warren this year and the reasons are variations on the same sentiments. 'It is a family area. It is quieter, more upmarket,' say Mark and Sue Perros. Both are aged 27 and their first child is on the way. This is their second home, having moved from Cranbourne. It is where they want to settle with their family. 'We will be here a long time,' they say.

It is the family zone. It is where people build dream homes – their first, second or third. It is the place to raise a family with two parents, two incomes and two cars.

The other drawcard is the regional package: relatives and work close by and value-for-money house and land deals. Newlyweds and newly settled Nicole and John Whiteside say they have family and friends in the area and they work close by. Both in their 20s, they say they will start a family in a few years 'and we will still be here'. [...]

And, it seems, the suburb doesn't disappoint families. Dianna and David Horskins bought their Narre Warren block of land in 1985 two years before they married, 'when it was affordable and there were still cows'. It did feel a long way away then, 'but dollars were the big thing'. But now other suburbs have caught them and stretched beyond and they are no longer the fringe.

Now, with two children at the local primary school, they have everything they want: 'We can walk to school from our house, walk to the shopping centre. There is nothing out of reach for general everyday living. There are plenty of activities here ... It is new but there is part of Narre Warren that is old enough that all the facilities are here. We are not limited because we are in a newer area.'

As for the ever-growing housing estates, well, it's a pity it couldn't all stay cows and daisies, but they knew one day it would imitate the Glen Waverley of David's childhood. And anyway, says Dianna, 'Five minutes down that road we are at the foothills of the Dandenongs, so it's not as if we can't escape suburbia'.

It is from these foothills that Narre Warren takes its name – Narree Narree, the Aboriginal word for the district, meaning small hills.
The council is aware of the need to protect the green and coastal areas of the region from the

ferocious demand for new 300-acre housing estates, for without these the area would become a wasteland of featureless rooftops.

But the sheer volume of the families moving into Casey is awesome, as is the demand they carry with them. It is the third largest growing municipality in Australia. About 2300 four-year-olds go to kindergarten in Casey. About 15,000 residents are aged under five years. There are 40 private and four council-run local child-care centres. Four new schools are needed. Looking at display homes is a big weekend activity. [...]

So while there is enough land and appeal, the push will continue. Casey is expected to be Victoria's biggest municipality just after the turn of the century, peaking eventually at a population of 320,000.

1 *fertile* (adj) ['fɜːtaɪl ☆ 'fɜːrtl]: (of land or soil) that plants can grow well in **2** lush: covered in healthy grass and plants • *housing estate:* area in which a large number of houses are planned and built together **4** *rooftile:* (Dach)ziegel **5** *municipality:* city, town or district which has its own local government **6** *fringe* [frɪndʒ]: outer edge of an area or group **7** *suburb:* area where people live that is outside a city centre **11** *Narre Warren:* outer area of Melbourne **13** *upmarket* (adj): designed for or used by people of a higher income-level **16** *Cranbourne:* outer area of Melbourne **23** *drawcard:* (here) attraction **25** *newlywed* (n): person who has been recently married, or wed **34–35** *affordable:* that can be bought or paid for **50** *daisy:* wildflower with a yellow center and white petals **54** *Dandenongs:* range of foothills east of Melbourne **61** *ferocious* (adj): very strong; fierce **65** *awesome:* very impressive; remarkable **72** *display* (adj): for exhibition or presentation **77** *peak:* reach a maximum

A sea of rooftops in one of Australia's growing suburban areas

1. What makes the suburbs of Casey and Narre Warren particularly attractive to young families?
2. What potential problem do the local councils face (cf. ll. 59–63)?
3. Sum up the pros and cons involved in living in the expanding suburbs of Melbourne.
4. How do the writers make use of quotes and statistical facts and what effect do they have?
5. How does life in Casey and Narre Warren, as described in the article, compare with the area in which you live? Which seems preferable to you as a place to live and why?
6. Working in groups, research the Internet to find out how living patterns (the numbers of people living in big cities, small towns and in the countryside or outback) are changing in Australia. Compare your results with the other groups.

5 A Sports Star Nicholas Jose

In his novel *The Custodians* (1997), author Nicholas Jose offers a sharp study of Australia's people, looking at common questions of identity and sense of place through the lives of present-day Australians. At the centre of the story is Cleve Gordon, a young Aborigine who was taken forcefully from his family by the government Welfare office and raised by a white family. The following are scenes from Cleve's youth.

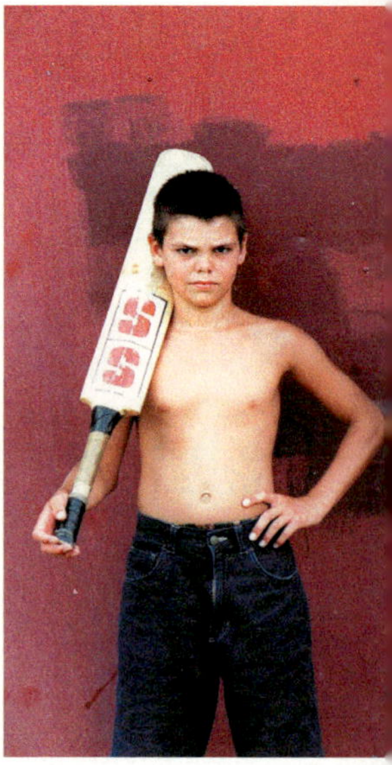

Cleve Gordon couldn't help but get himself noticed. He was a spirited kid. That was why his foster parents had chosen him from the orphanage when he was three years old. By the time he was twelve, he was an altar boy, wearing the dress and hanging round with the old priest in the country town where they lived. That was how he got the scholarship to St Joeys. Cleve knew how things worked. The Adamses, who had taken Cleve in as an act of thanks to God when their daughter's leukemia was cured, were proud to send him off to boarding school with the Brothers in the city, feeling they had done their duty. The scholarship provided sports gear and hand-me-down clothes, plus food and board – but no cash to call your own. It was that sort of scholarship.

The best time at school was training, when you could show how good you were. Cleve could fight his way out of most situations, but when sometimes he ended up moping in corners for a couple of days and the boys caught him having a cry, no one said anything. If it had been one of them, they would have jeered without mercy. Only if Cleve missed a moment during training would they taunt him. 'Gone walkabout, Choco,' they yelled. Cleve laughed. They were not his own people. Everyone knew that, but no one ever said anything.

The school emptied on weekends. On Saturdays, after the match, the place went quiet. Most boarders had relatives in the city and money to go out by themselves. That was when Cleve invited the mob from the square to come and visit him. An uncle who came into town from the riverland drove them all out to the school in his old car. They got lost on the way and lost again inside the school grounds, driving round and round looking for someone to ask. The highest spot Cleve could find to keep lookout for them was up the fire ladder at the top of the chapel spire from where the city of Adelaide looked like a patterned green carpet. Squatting dizzily on the raked tiles, the boy could see across to the flat shiny sea. Then he saw the car turning in a loop around the lawn below. He hollered out three times until the mob heard him. Sticking their heads out the car windows, they cast their eyes up in astonishment.

Brother Gavin was waiting for Cleve at the bottom of the fire ladder, ready to lead the gaggle of visitors to the staffroom for a pot of tea.

'The boy's doing all right, eh Brother?' asked one of the aunties, speaking on behalf of all Cleve's friends from the square. They were making sure he was all right. But after they had gone, Brother Gavin gave Cleve a thrashing. He should think about the consequences of what he did. He might have fallen off the chapel roof. He should not invite strangers to the school. He should not take the law into his own hands.

The people never visited Cleve again after that. If he was going to have a proper education, he was better off obeying all the rules anyway. He was better off left the way he was going.

As a sports star, Cleve had privileged status at St Joeys. On weekends, when he was hanging around school by himself, the Brothers would kick a ball with him, or play serious cricket. In return Cleve was expected to put in the full complement of appearances at Mass. They talked of the day when Cleve would be a holy man like them.

One time Garry Adams, the class captain, invited Cleve home to his birthday party in the suburbs. Cleve borrowed a set of good clothes for the occasion. Garry's father, a pharmacist, had organised a barbecue. The Adamses, country people originally, had worked with the Mastermans, the big pastoralists, in the old days. Elspeth Gillingham's mother had been a Masterman, so Elspeth was at the party too, and Sophie and Robbie Masterman, Elspeth's country cousins. The Adamses were Catholic and the Mastermans Protestant but despite the sectarian divide, and the political differences that went with it, the families kept up the association because of old land ties. Cleve was part of that too. It was other Adamses, Garry's uncle and aunt, who had fostered him. That made him a sort of cousin, although no one thought of Cleve in that way.

They were playing cricket in the backyard. Garry had told Robbie that Cleve was a top sportsman and Robbie was determined to test him. Cleve bowled and Robbie puffed up his cheeks and frowned, prepared to smash. Cleve gave him some easy balls to hit to start off with, although hard to score runs from. Then when Robbie was starting to feel confident, Cleve delivered a ball that bowled him clean through the middle stump and Robbie was out for a duck.

'Good one, Choco,' said Garry, embarrassed for Robbie, who was the oldest boy there.

'Shit, I didn't even see it coming,' said Robbie, unable to look Cleve in the eye. 'Who's he training with?'

'Under 15s.' Cleve answered for himself.

'Fuck that for a joke,' swore Robbie. 'I bet they lost the birth certificate.'

Elspeth, who was wicketkeeper, found the ball in the back of the garden and came loping back with it. She was pleased to see her uncouth cousin cut down to size. She tossed the ball neatly back to Cleve, who plucked it from the air, bowing his head as he returned to his mark.

When the food was ready, they sat around on the grass eating their grilled chops and sausages in their fingers. Garry's mother passed Cleve extra helpings, saying he needed feeding up. Even the birthday cake, after the coloured candles were picked off, was cut so as to allow one extra piece for Cleve.

'It's not fair,' declared Elspeth. 'Why should he be treated differently?'

'Don't forget who's a visitor,' warned Mrs Adams. 'Family hold back.'

'I'm not family either,' said Elspeth. She passed the last piece to Cleve.

'I'll halve it with you,' Cleve grinned to her. 'I'm family too, Mrs Adams. Don't forget.'

Mrs Adams laughed. 'That's right, Cleve dear. You're family too.'

While they sat on the grass, the kids compared their smallpox vaccination marks. Mr Adams explained that the size of the mark depended on the age at which a child was inoculated. Mr Adams talked about the way immunisation programs were organised across the country and around the world, like a net, to catch everyone, until in the end contagious diseases would disappear from the earth. As a pharmacist, he looked forward to that day, even if it would be bad for his business. But that did not explain why Cleve had a whole string of vaccination marks down his arm.

'What happened to you, Cleve?' asked Mr Adams.

Cleve said that according to his foster mother all the vaccines were trialled on him in the orphanage. Elspeth shuddered when she looked at the five rings of pale stretched skin on Cleve's arm. Mr Adams said how wonderful it would be if Cleve could become a doctor one day himself.

Cleve shook his head. 'Too much study.'

'He's going to be a football champion,' said Garry. 'That's what he's got to be.'

'I wouldn't mind being an astronaut, actually,' said Cleve and they all laughed.

Elspeth was picked up from the birthday party by her father. Dr Gillingham sat outside and watched the kids come out. Once his daughter was in the car, he asked who the dark boy was.

'He's a scholarship kid from St Joeys,' said Elspeth. 'He's an Aborigine,' she clarified.

'They must have brought him down from the river to be in their football team,' commented her father.

Angus Gillingham mentioned it to his wife later. 'There was an Abo at the kids' party. Do you think it's a good idea? For Elspeth, I mean. She gets funny ideas. Micks and Abos,' he snorted. 'There's a limit, isn't there? Did you have any idea?'

'It's good for her,' Barb Gillingham replied. 'Why does it bother you?'

'I think the Adamses should have warned us, that's all. You can carry mixing too far. Elspeth's only a girl.'

'Nothing's going to rub off on Elspeth, darling,' his wife laughed. 'Her lasting friendships will be with her own kind.'

2 *foster parent:* adult who gives parental care to another person's child, without becoming his or her legal parent **3** *orphanage:* home for children whose parents are dead **4** *altar boy:* boy who assists a priest at a Christian mass

6 *scholarship:* Stipendium **8** *leukemia* (AE) = (BE) *leukaemia* [luː'kiːmiə]: serious disease of the blood which causes weakness and sometimes death **8–9** *boarding school:* school where children can live during the term/semester

10 *hand-me-down* (AE) = (BE) *cast-off:* (of clothes) second-hand **14** *mope:* Trübsal blasen **16** *jeer:* laugh at sb. or shout rude remarks to show that you do not respect them **17** *taunt sb.* [tɔːnt]: try to make sb. angry or upset by saying unkind things, laughing at their failures, etc. • *walkabout* (AustE): (of Aborigines) temporary return to traditional life, taken especially between periods of work or residence in white society and usually involving a period of walking through the bush **21** *mob* [mɒb ☆ mɑːb]: disorderly crowd **26** *spire:* tall pointed structure on the top of a building, esp. a church

27 *squat:* sit on your heels with your knees bent up close to your body • *raked* (adj): placed on a slope (= Schräge) **29** *holler out:* yell or shout

32 *gaggle* (n): group of noisy people

36 *thrashing* (n): severe beating **45** *cricket:* game played on grass by two teams of 11 players; players score points (called 'runs') by hitting a ball with a wooden bat and running between two sets of upright wooden sticks, called 'stumps' **46** *full complement of sth.:* complete number or quantity of sth. needed or wanted **51** *pharmacist:* Apothekerin, Apotheker • *barbecue* (n): grill party **53** *pastoralist:* farmer who raises and herds cows, sheep, etc. **56** *despite:* trotz • *sectarian divide:* difference between groups of people who have different religious views **62** *bowl:* (of cricket) throw a ball towards the batsman **63** *puff sth. up:* blow sth. up with air **64** *score runs:* (of cricket) make points; cf. also *cricket*, l. 45 **66** *stump:* cf. *cricket*, l. 45 • *be out for a duck:* (of cricket) fail to hit the ball with the bat and score any runs (cf. also *cricket*, l. 45) **73** *wicketkeeper:* (of cricket) player positioned immediately behind the wicket (= either of the two *stumps* [cf. *cricket*, l. 45] with a piece of wood resting on top) **74** *lope:* run with long relaxed steps • *uncouth* [ʌn'kuːθ]: (of a person or their behaviour) rude or socially unacceptable

87 *smallpox:* Pocken • *vaccination:* Impfung **89** *inoculate sb.:* jm. impfen **91** *contagious:* (of an illness or disease) transmitted by people touching each other **96–97** *trial sth. on sb.:* test sth. on sb. **113** *Abo* (sl) (derog): Aboriginal person **115** *Mick* (sl) (derog): Irish or Roman Catholic person **123** *rub off on sb.:* (of personal qualities, behaviour, opinions, etc.) become part of sb.'s character as a result of that person spending time with sb. with those qualities

1. Why is sport important to Cleve and how does it affect his relationship with the other boys at his school (cf. ll. 12–18)?

2. How does Cleve handle the events at Garry Adams's birthday party?

3. How do Garry Adams's and Elspeth Gillingham's parents differ in their attitudes towards Cleve? Give examples to explain your answer.

4. Judging from this excerpt, what sort of person is Cleve? Write a personal profile, using examples from the text. Discuss your results.

5. Describe the perspective from which the narrator tells the story. What makes this point of view effective?

6. Do you think Cleve is unfairly discriminated against in any of the situations described in the text? Use examples to explain your answer.

7. What effect do you think Cleve's unusual situation in life might have on his identity and sense of self? What advantages or disadvantages might his experiences have for him in terms of his personal development?

Whose Country Is It?

1 Tracks in the Outback

As the 2000 Olympic Games in Sydney showed, interest in traditional Aboriginal culture – the art, the oral history, the special relationship to nature – has grown immensely. Enterprising Aboriginal tour companies take large numbers of tourists each year to sites of natural beauty and indigenous life in the outback. The collision of world views which such a visit can bring is more than many tourists come prepared for. Here is an account of one outback tour, taken from an Australian travel magazine.

Ancient spirits on cave walls in Kakadu National Park, Northern Territory (above); visitors explore Uluru (opposite above); a tour guide demonstrates bush survival skills (opposite below).

On the surface, the Desert Tracks Cave Hill tour is a leisurely affair. It starts with a sunrise breakfast overlooking Mount Connor, a mesa-shaped mountain east of Uluru. Then a quick run down to Mulga Park station for a cuppa with the station's owners and a chat about life in the district.

It's mid-morning before we reach Cave Hill itself and meet our Aboriginal guide for the day, Dickie Minyintiri. At best, his English could be described as creative, yet he displays a down-to-earth humour. Over yet another cup of tea, he starts talking, asking questions, demonstrating a few bush skills. Around him, lawyers and journalists have itchy feet. Where are the cave paintings? When are we going to start doing things? We still haven't got the point.

Lunch is served. Dickie keeps talking. How long we are staying? he asks. 'One day,' he exclaims, shaking his head. 'Not long enough.' His disappointment is unambiguous. What can we possibly expect to learn about his culture in such a short time? If it were up to him, we'd spend the afternoon drinking tea, talking, relaxing, de-stressing, getting to know each other. Then we might be ready to be receptive to what he is trying to teach us about his country.

After we've eaten, though, we set off to the hill itself to look at the cave paintings. Along the way, Dickie points out bushfoods and emphasises the importance of not taking photos, then begins to tell the story whose drama is played out in this area. By the time we reach the cave itself we have the thread of the tale of Wati Niru and the two sisters. Inside, the ceiling of the cave is like a giant story-book, tracing Niru's pursuit of the women. To trick them, he changes himself into the bushfoods and landforms now used by Aboriginal people.

Dickie tells only the men's part of the story, which gets pretty racy in places. It seems Niru was pretty well endowed, a point that seems to impress Dickie, who is harping on it. Slowly it occurs to us that it's a feature of his story-telling – he repeats everything often, committing what is purely oral story to your memory. To paraphrase Lewis Carroll, "What I tell you three times, you'll remember."

Afterwards he takes us to the top of the hill. The view is stupendous across vast open country north-east to Mount Connor, east to Mount Woodruff (the highest in South Australia and home of the Perenti dreaming) and north-west to the distant outline of Uluru itself. Dotting the hill are small permanent waterholes and another tiny cave opening (through which the women escaped Wati Niru).

Dickie's storytelling links these and the features around us into a growing understanding of his land. Back at the *wiltja* (shelter), there's just time for another cuppa and

for Dickie to remonstrate with us some more about not spending enough time, to slow down in order to take it all in. He even takes one of the lawyers aside and talks with her for some time, drawing symbols in the dust between them. It turns out he's trying to talk her into becoming one of his wives, a forlorn hope we think as we sip our tea and muse on the Pitjantjatjara word for lesbian.

Later, after a truly bone-jarring 'scenic' drive, we decline the chance to see yet another Uluru sunset. Instead, we ask if we can stop at Mutitjulu Waterhole, at the base of the rock. As we arrive, the last bus group is hurrying away to the sunset viewing area and we have the place to ourselves. And there, at the end of our day, we sit in silence.

Cooler air is starting to come, dropping down through the day's heat, mixing with the smell of the bush. We listen to the birds, watch the last sunlight slide off the upper reaches of the rock, soak up the atmosphere and feel as though at least some of Dickie's message has gotten through.

1. Why do the people who have joined the Desert Tracks Cave Hill tour have 'itchy feet' (l. 15)?
2. What point is Dickie Minyintiri, the Aboriginal guide, trying to make to the tourists?
3. What does the writer mean when he or she says that 'On the surface, the ... tour is a leisurely affair' (ll. 1–2)?
4. In your view, what is the main feature of this tour and why?
5. What are some notable differences between people of traditional cultures like the Aborigines and people of modern industrialized cultures in terms of their views of life? Which perspectives do you sympathize with most and why?
6. Discuss the possible positive and negative effects of tourism on the area described in the text. Consider its impact on the local people, the environment, the economy, the lifestyle, etc. Find another example of a place in the world in which tourism is controversial and make a list of the similarities and differences.

1 *desert:* Wüste **2** *leisurely* ['leʒə- ☆ 'li:ʒər-] (adj): done without hurrying **3–4** *mesa-shaped* ['meɪsə]: having a form like a *mesa*, a hill with a flat top and steep sides, common in the southwest of the USA **4** *Uluru:* world's largest stone and the most famous landmark in Australia's outback (see the photos, p. 43), also known as Ayers Rock **5** *cuppa* (BE infml): cup of sth., usually tea **11–12** *down-to-earth:* straightforward, realistic; sensible **14** *bush skills:* techniques for surviving in the bush, an area of wild land in Australia or Africa **15** *have itchy feet:* be restless or nervous **15–16** *cave painting:* Höhlenmalerei **21** *unambiguous:* clear in meaning **26** *receptive to sth.:* willing to receive sth. favourably **34** *thread* [θred]: thin string made of cotton, wool, etc. used for sewing; idea that connects the different parts of sth. (e.g. a story) **35** *ceiling* ['si:l-]: (Zimmer)decke **36** *trace sth.:* describe a process or development of sth. **41** *racy:* exciting and entertaining, sometimes in a way that is connected with sex **42** *well endowed:* having a large penis **43** *harp on (about) sth.:* talk about sth. to an excessive degree **47** *Lewis Carroll* (1832-1898): English author, best known for his fantasy *Alice's Adventures in Wonderland* (1865) **50** *stupendous:* extremely large or impressive
53 *dreaming* (n): Aboriginal concept of the creation of the world; story told about this process **65** *remonstrate with sb. about sth.* ['remən- ☆ rɪ'mɑ:n-] (fml): protest or complain about sb./sth. **71** *forlorn:* nearly hopeless **72** *muse on sth.* [mju:z]: think carefully about sth. for a time • *Pitjantjatjara:* language of the Aboroginal people of the same name of northern South Australia **74** *bone-jarring* (adj): characterized by hard jerky movements which cause physical dis-comfort **86** *soak sth. up:* absorb sth. into your senses, body or mind

Visitor at an Aborigine camp, 1930

2 The Only Way of Dealing with Blacks David Malouf

David Malouf is one of Australia's most celebrated authors. In his novel *Remembering Babylon* (1994), Gemmy Fairly is a 19th-century English sailor who is shipwrecked on the Queensland coast. He is rescued by Aborigines who give him a new home. Many years later he leaves them to join a white settlement, and there he sees his old countrymen with different eyes. In the following extract he meets with some of the men.

From the beginning there were those among them, Ned Corcoran was the most vehement, for whom the only way of dealing with blacks was the one that had been given scope elsewhere. 'We ought to go out,' he insisted, controlling the spit that flooded his mouth, 'and get rid of 'em, once and for all. If I catch one of the buggers round my place, I'll fuckin' pot 'im.' He jerked out the last couple of syllables, and the explosion they made, and the silence afterwards, made some men uncomfortably hot. The rest shifted their boots but did not speak. They were not so candid as Ned Corcoran, but did not essentially disagree with him. It was the quickest way; the kindest too maybe, in the long run. They had seen what happened to blacks in places where the locals were kind. It wasn't a pleasant sight.

But there were others, the milder members of the settlement, who argued that it was surely worth trying a softer policy. What they looked forward to was a settled space in which they could get on with the hard task of founding a home, and maybe, if they were lucky, a town where in time all the civilities would prevail. If they got the preliminaries right, the natives too might be drawn in, as labourers, or house-servants. They had secretly, some of them, a vision of plantations with black figures moving in rows down a field, a compound with neat whitewashed huts, a hallway, all polished wood, with an old grey-haired black saying 'Yessir', and preparing to pull off their boots (all this off in the future of course, maybe far off; for the moment they would not mention the boots since most of them did not have any). They ought at least, so they thought, to use this Gemmy fellow to get some reliable information that would temper with fact the fantastic rumours that flew about the place and kept them in a state of permanent anxiety. What haunted them was the endless round of reprisals they would be involved in if one of their number got jumped and speared (as God knows could happen easily enough) and some hot-head like Ned Corcoran took it into his head to get up an extermination party.

So from the beginning his questioners, Gemmy saw, were of two kinds. One lot wanted to make an ally of him in what they hoped would be an easy war.

They were affable, these fellows. They offered him chews of tobacco, squatted on their heels, and hummed and harred and looked off into the distance – he had a good idea what they were seeing there. They fished about, first one, then another, in a casual way, for what they wanted to know: whether the tribes, out there, up there, were in the habit of gathering at any one particular spot, and in what numbers, and if it was just the men or the whole mob of them, women and children as well. They chewed their tobacco and shot out the juice, or quietly smoked, with no urgency in them; but he felt the purpose in their hands, saw in their eyes the volleys of grey smoke spreading, then hanging like rain. They chuckled to themselves and thought he could not hear. He chewed his tobacco and was still.

When he first came among them he had been unable to tell from their wooden expressions, and the even more wooden gestures, what they had in their heads. They hid what they felt as if they were ashamed of it, or so he had decided; though whether in front of others or before themselves, he could not tell. Their eyes, their mouths, seemed dead in the rigid faces.

3 *scope* (n) (U): opportunity to function **5** *bugger* (sl) (vulg): offensive word used to insult sb., esp. a man, and to show anger or dislike • *pot sb./sth.:* shoot sb./sth. **8** *candid:* saying what you think openly and honestly **15** *civility* (fml): polite behaviour **16** *prevail* (fml): be accepted, esp. after a struggle or argument • *preliminary* (n): event that precedes the main action **19** *compound:* area surrounded by a fence or wall in which a group of buildings stands **23** *reliable* [rɪ'laɪəbl]: that can be trusted **24** *temper sth. with sth.* (fml): make sth. less extreme by adding sth. that has the opposite effect **26** *haunt sb.:* (of an unpleasant thought) keep coming to sb.'s mind so that they cannot forget it • *reprisal:* Vergeltungsmaßnahme **27** *jump sb.* (infml): attack sb. suddenly **29** *extermination:* act of getting rid of sth. by destroying it completely • *party:* group of people who are doing sth. together **31** *ally* ['ælaɪ]: person who helps and supports sb. in a difficult position **33** *affable:* easy and pleasant to speak to **34** *hum and har* (usu. *haw*) (infml): take a long time to make a decision or before you say sth. **41** *volley* (n): a lot of sth. (esp. bullets, stones, etc.) that are shot or thrown at the same time **42** *chuckle:* laugh quietly or to oneself **48** *rigid* ['rɪdʒɪd]: stiff, unmoving

1. How do the men in the group react to Ned Corcoran's views on how to deal with the Aboriginal people?
2. What do the men want from Gemmy?
3. How does Gemmy interpret the 'wooden expressions' (l. 45) of his counterparts?
4. Find some further instances of body language in the text. What is the author telling the reader about these people?
5. Describe the perspective of the narrator in this excerpt. Why do you think the author has chosen this point of view?
6. Malouf's story takes place in 19th-century Australia. To what extent do you think attitudes like those described here exist in today's world? Explain, using your own examples.
7. Look at the photo on these two pages of a landscape in the outback. Draw some associations between the text you have just read and this picture.

3 Unrecorded Battlefields Henry Reynolds

Henry Reynold's critical perspective on Australia's history is well-known and provocative among his fellow white historians. In his study and documentation of white settlement on the continent, the historian and Aboriginal rights activist tells the untold and often painful stories of Australia's colonial past. The following is an excerpt from Reynold's book *Frontier – Reports from the Edge of White Settlement* (1996).

Was Australia settled or invaded? pioneered or conquered? won by sweat or won by blood? Was it the fruit of industry or a prize of war? These are questions which have reverberated through Australian history, the cause of argument and anguish since the early years of settlement. One of the first histories of New South Wales, published in 1816, expressed the view that colonisation in the antipodes was uniquely peaceful:

for here there are no scenes ... of desolating war and bloodshed to contemplate, no peaceable inhabitants driven from their smiling dwellings, and deprived of the comforts of life, by means of the destroying invader. Our settlers have not established themselves by the sword, nor willingly done injury to the naked miserable stragglers, who were found on these barren shores.

It was an appealing interpretation of colonial history which gained many followers. Writing half a century later, at a time of escalating frontier conflict, Queensland's Governor Bowen hailed the 'triumph of peaceful progress ... victories without injustice or bloodshed, conquests not over man, but over nature'.

The opposing view of colonisation was strongly argued in a letter written to a Launceston paper in 1831 at the end of three years of intense conflict with the Tasmanian Aborigines. The correspondent, J.E., asked rhetorically:

> Are these unhappy people, the subjects of our King, in a state of rebellion or are they an injured people, whom we have invaded and with whom we are at war?
>
> Are they within the reach of our laws; or are they to be judged by the law of nations? Are they to be viewed in the light of murderers, or as prisoners of war?
>
> Have they been guilty of any crime under the laws of nations which is punishable by death, or have they only been carrying on a war in their way?
>
> Are they British subjects at all, or a foreign enemy who has never yet been subdued and which resists our usurped authority and domination ...
>
> We are at war with them: they look upon us as enemies – as invaders – as oppressors and persecutors – they resist our invasion. They have never been subdued, therefore they are not rebellious subjects, but an injured nation, defending in their own way, their rightful possessions, which have been torn from them by force.

Colonial mounted soldiers and Aborigines at battle in Western Australia in the early 19th century (W.L. Walton, 1852)

The legal situation was clear from the beginning. Australia was a colony of settlement not of conquest. The common law arrived with the First Fleet; the Aborigines became instant subjects of the King, amenable to, and in theory protected by, that law. They could be murdered, outlawed or made subject to martial law but they could not be treated as enemies of the state. Lord Glenelg, the Secretary of State for the Colonies, issued a definitive statement of the situation in 1837 when informing Governor Bourke that the blacks were protected by the law and that it was impossible to regard them as aliens 'with whom a war can exist, and against whom Her Majesty's troops may exercise belligerent rights'. But few of those who had lived on the frontier thought of Australia as a uniquely peaceful society, legal theory or historical interpretation notwithstanding. Neither theory nor interpretation could satisfactorily account for the violence which haunted the pioneer fringe for 150 years. Writing in 1880, the ethnographers Fison and Howitt summed up the experience of a century of conflict:

> It may be stated broadly that the advance of settlement has, upon the frontier at least, been marked by a line of blood. The actual conflict of the two races has varied in intensity and in duration, as the various native tribes have themselves in mental and physical character ... But the tide of settlement has advanced along an ever widening line, breaking the tribes with its first waves and overwhelming their wrecks with its flood.

Was it warfare?

Frontier skirmishing felt like a form of warfare. Those who had experienced it said so in books and newspapers, letters and speeches, in public statement and private conversations, in every colony and throughout the nineteenth century. Before the settlement at Sydney was a year old, Governor Phillip and his officers were complaining about a 'state of petty warfare'; an 'open war' started with Hawkesbury River clans as the settlers began to farm the valley in 1795. In 1826, with the Europeans edging along the Hunter River, the missionary L.E. Threlkeld wrote home to England: 'You will be grieved to hear that war has commenced and still continues against the Aborigines of this land.' Two years later a troubled Tasmanian settler wrote to the Governor with suggestions about how to 'stop the ferocious warfare which now reigns in this Island'; a week later the Governor himself communicated with all the magistrates deploring the 'lawless and cruel warfare'. A naval captain visiting the Swan River in 1832 noted in his diary that there was 'really a most awful warfare' in progress; a pioneer West Australian settler declared: 'We are at war with the original owners, we have never known them in any capacity but as enemies.' In northern New South Wales in the late 1830s Europeans felt they were 'in an enemy's country'; the whole region was in 'a state of warfare'. Twenty years later the Queensland parliament heard that the colonists 'must be considered to be, as they always have been, at open war with the Aborigines'. In 1879 the editor of the Queenslander informed his readers: 'we are today at open war with every tribe of wild blacks on the frontier'; a colleague writing for the Queensland Figaro referred to the 'constant border warfare on the verge line of settlement'. Blacks killed by the Queensland Native Police, a parliamentary committee was told, 'were shot in battle' on what a retired officer of the force termed 'the unrecorded battlefields of Queensland'.

Martyrs of their country

While Europeans often attributed Aboriginal resistance to their adversaries' savage nature, there were many settlers who regarded it as the natural, if unwelcome, response to invasion. 'They consider every injury they can inflict upon white men as an act of duty and patriotic [sic],' a Tasmanian colonist wrote in 1828, 'and however they may dread the punishment which our laws inflict upon them, they consider the sufferers ... as martyrs of their country.' A contemporary wrote to a Hobart paper two years later observing that every day afforded 'some proof of their determination to destroy, and their declaration to war with the whites'. It was absurd to see the blacks 'in the light of occasional rioters', a New South Wales settler argued in 1839; they were 'enemies arrayed in arms and waging war against Europeans as their invaders'. A visitor to the colony in the 1840s argued: 'It must not be forgotten, while we are meditating on the treatment of the natives ... that their country is occupied by force – that they attempted, but in vain, to beat off the English settlers.' The editor of the Northern Territory Times remarked in 1875: 'We are invading their country and they have a perfect right to – and it is but natural that they should – do their best to obstruct our passage through it.'

1 *invade sth.:* enter sth. (a country, town, etc.) using military force in order to take control of it **3** *reverberate* [-'---] (fml): have a strong effect on people for a long time **6** *the antipodes* [æn'tɪpədi:z] (BE) (pl): way of referring to Australia and New Zealand, often used in a humorous way • *unique* (adj): very special or unusual **7** *desolating* (adj): sad and without hope **7–8** *contemplate sth.:* consider sth. carefully and at length **8** *dwelling* (n): place to live in **9** *deprive sb. of sth.:* take sth. away from sb. **11** *straggler:* person or animal that is among the last or slowest in a group to do sth. • *barren* (adj): not producing anything useful or successful **13** *appealing* (adj): attractive or interesting **15** *hail sth.:* salute or greet sth. **16** *conquest:* Eroberung, Sieg **19** *Launceston:* city in Tasmania **22** *injured* (adj): physically or emotionally hurt **30** *subdue sb./sth.* (fml): bring sb./sth. under control, esp. by using force • *usurp sth.* [ju:'zɜ:p]: take sth. (esp. someone else's power, position, job, etc.) when you do not have the right to **32** *persecutor* ['----]: Verfolgerin, Verfolger **37** *First Fleet:* group of British ships that brought the first settlers to Australia in 1788 (cf. Info-Box, p. 18) **38** *amenable to sth.* [ə'mi:nəbl]: (of people) willing to be influenced by sth. **40** *martial law:* Kriegsrecht **45** *belligerent* [-dʒ-]: unfriendly and aggressive • *the frontier* (sing): edge of land where people live and have built towns, beyond which the country is wild and unknown **47** *notwithstanding* (prep) (fml): trotz **48** *haunt sb./sth.:* continue to cause problems to sb./sth. for a long time • *fringe* [frɪndʒ]: outer edge of an area or group **53** *duration* (fml): length of time that sth. lasts or continues **58** *skirmishing* (n): act of taking part in a short fight or argument **62** *petty:* of small importance **64** *edge* (v): move slowly and carefully in a particular direction **65** *grieve sb.* (fml): make sb. feel very sad **73–74** *capacity:* Form **81** *verge line:* (here) outer edge or border **86** *attribute sth. to sth.:* relate sth. (an event) to sth. (a particular cause) • *adversary* ['----] (fml): enemy, opponent **87** *savage* ['sævɪdʒ]: angry and violent; causing great harm **90** *dread sth.* [dred]: be very afraid of sth. **95** *rioter:* person who behaves violently in a public place, usu. as a protest **96** *array sb./sth.* (fml): place sb./sth. in a certain order **102** *obstruct sth.:* block, prevent sth.

1. Describe the two opposing views in the 19th century about the progress of early colonisation in Australia (cf. ll. 4–35).
2. According to Reynolds, how was the situation in the colonies defined under British common law (cf. ll. 36–45)?
3. How did the experiences of the colonists contradict the official view of things (cf. ll. 87–102)?
4. Explain the metaphor which the ethnographers Fison and Howitt use in lines 54–56 to describe the conflict. Think of another metaphor that would also fit in this context.
5. Discuss the attitude of the colonists when they introduced 'common law' (l. 37) to the continent. What is your personal reaction to their way of seeing things?
6. According to the text, some settlers showed understanding towards the Aborigines. Using the information and quotes in ll. 85–102, write a poem from the perspective of one such settler.

Two Histories and the Process of Reconciliation

*Aboriginal and Torres Strait Islander people are collectively referred to here as 'Aborigines', while it is acknowledged that the Torres Strait Islanders have their own separate cultures, histories and languages.

Although Australia's indigenous people, the Aborigines and Torres Strait Islanders*, arrived on the continent thousands of years before white colonisation, their place in Australia's history has been, until recent times, either played down or ignored completely.

Australia's past, it would seem, only began with Captain Cook's visit in 1770, the convict settlements which followed, and the increasing arrival of free settlers, explorers, gold miners and diverse peoples from all over the world. The British based their claim to Australia on the grounds that the continent was 'terra nullius' – a land belonging to no-one and thus ready for the taking.

British Common Law was instituted with the arrival of the First Fleet in 1788, which meant that land could be taken from the Aborigines without compensation. White settlement was all the more efficient since the concept of private land ownership was completely foreign to the indigenous people. In their view, land did not belong to individuals, but rather, people belonged to the land, were formed by it and were a part of it like everything else.

As a result, two histories of Australia exist, and many events which non-indigenous people celebrate as great moments in their history are a reason for sadness or anger to Aboriginal people. Up to the 1960s, before Aborigines were finally recognised as Australian citizens with equal rights, white historians were often openly racist in their descriptions of Aborigines. Some plainly ignored indigenous culture, which suffered brutal treatment and great loss through the white invasion.

The extent of resistance by Aborigines to the arrival of Europeans was also largely undocumented, thus creating the impression that Australia was taken peacefully by the British (see Text 3 in this chapter). Where Aboriginal resistance was mentioned at all, it was as acts of trespassing, thieving or killing rather than in terms of people defending their homes and their families.

As it became clear that Europeans were there to stay, many Aborigines accepted employment by the white settlers. They were often subjected to harsh, difficult and dangerous work conditions and were mostly underpaid.

The stolen generations

One of the worst chapters in relations between indigenous and non-indigenous Australians is the issue of the 'stolen children'. From the early 1800s onwards most Australian states and territories carried out a policy of forcibly removing Aboriginal children from their parents and placing them in institutions or foster families. These children were kept separate from their culture, in the hope that

Aborigines taken prisoner in Western Australia around 1900

they would lose their Aboriginality and eventually assimilate into white society. In 1849, a member of the New South Wales Committee on the Aborigines and Protectorate commented:

'The only method that could be adopted for the instruction and improvement of the natives is, in my opinion, to take away their children to some establishment where they would be entirely removed from the influence of their parents and tribe. [...] This, in my opinion, is the only means of saving the race from extermination.' (From: Rosalie Triolo, *The Australian Experience*, ABC, Cambridge, 1996, p. 11)

The indigenous child welfare system, as it was officially called, continued to function up to the 1970s. Few records were kept of children's origins and others were lost or destroyed. Today thousands of Aborigines know little about their original families and tribes. The issue has become a major hurdle in efforts to improve relations between indigenous and non-indigenous Australians. While attention has focused more and more on the tragedy, the government has been slow to acknowledge its past wrongs. In 2000 the Howard government apologized for questioning facts about the stolen generations, but by the end of 2001 it had still refused to issue a formal apology to those whose lives were affected.

A man displays the Aborigine flag during a demonstration in 1988.

Rights and reconciliation

The work of Aboriginal and non-Aboriginal activists has done much to improve the rights of indigenous peoples. Two decisions by the Australian High Court have strengthened Aborigines' traditional land rights. In 1992 the High Court rejected the legal doctrine of terra nullius and ruled in the historic Mabo Case that native title existed before the arrival of the British. While mining and other industries reacted negatively to this decision, it was praised by Aborigines and the government of the day as an important step on the path to reconciliation. In response, the Native Title Act of 1993 was passed, which further recognizes and protects native land rights. In the 1996 Wik Case, the High Court ruled that indigenous groups may claim native title to land which the government has already leased to others for raising sheep and cattle. In such cases Aborigines may use the land as long as their activities do not conflict with those of the leaseholder. The question of compensation for other land once used by Aborigines is still being debated.

Aborigine women outside their low-income housing in Sydney

While progress has been made with Aboriginal rights, the social situation of Aborigines is extremely bad. On every social scale they suffer the greatest disadvantages: declining health conditions, limited access to education, the psychological and emotional torments of family separation, high rates of poverty and the highest unemployment rate among Australians.

Despite this, Aboriginal people are taking responsibility for their histories and their preservation to an extent greater than at any time since the arrival of Europeans. Their success in areas such as sport, music, film, theatre and dance has also helped create an awareness and market for Aboriginal culture that goes well beyond national borders.

of poetry, including *John Pat and Other Poems* (1988), from which the following is taken. This poem is a protest against the exclusion of Aborigines from the celebrations of 150 years of European settlement in Western Australia, 1829–1979.

I walked slowly along the river.
Old iron, broken concrete, rusted cans
scattered stark along the shore,
plastic strewn by man and tide
littered loudly mute on sparse growth
struggling to survive.
A flock of gulls quarrelled over debris,
a lone shag looked hopefully down at turgid water
and juggernauts of steel and stone made jigsaw
patterns against the city sky.

So now that the banners have fluttered,
the eulogies ended and the tattoos have rendered
the rattle of spears,
look back and remember the end of December
and one hundred and fifty years.

Three boys crackled past on trailbikes
long blond hair waving in the wind,
speedboats erupted power
while lesser craft surged along behind.
The breeze rustled a patch of bull-oak
reminding me of swan, bittern, wild duck winging –
now all alien to the river.
Sir John Forrest stood tall in stone
in St George's Terrace,
gun across shoulder,
Symbolic of what had removed
the river's first children.

And that other river, the Murray,
where Western Australia's
first mass murderer Captain Stirling,
trappings flashing, rode gaily
at the head of twenty-four men.
For an hour they fired
and bodies black, mutilated,
floated down the blood-stained stream.

So now that the banners have fluttered,
the eulogies ended and the tattoos have rendered
the rattle of spears,
look back and remember the end of December
and one hundred and fifty years.

2 *concrete* (n): Beton **3** *stark* (adj): unpleasant; real and impossible to avoid **5** *mute* [mju:t]: not speaking; silent • *sparse:* not thick or dense **7** *gull:* Möwe • *debris* ['debri: ☆ də'bri:]: pieces of wood, metal, etc., that are left after sth. has been broken or destroyed **8** *shag:* large black sea bird with a long neck **9** *juggernaut:* large and powerful force or institution that cannot be controlled; (here) large construction, e.g. an office building or a bridge • *jigsaw:* irregularly shaped, like a jigsaw puzzle **11** *flutter:* move lightly and quickly, e.g. in the wind **12** *eulogy* ['ju:lədʒi]: speech or piece of writing which praises sth. very much • *tattoo:* outdoor show by members of the armed forces that includes marching, music and military exercises • *render sth.* (fml): express or perform sth. **16** *crackle:* pass noisily **18** *erupt sth.:* throw out sth. suddenly and violently **19** *surge:* move quickly and forcefully in a particular direction **20** *bull-oak:* type of oak tree (= Eichen) which is native to Australia **21** *bittern:* type of water bird **23** *Sir John Forrest* (1847–1918): Australian statesman and explorer; first premier of Western Australia (1890–1901) **24** *St George's Terrace:* street in downtown Perth, Western Australia **28** *Murray = Murray River:* river in South Australia, east of the city of Adelaide **30** *Captain Stirling = Sir James Stirling* (1791–1865): British officer, founder and first Lieutenant-Governor (1828–1832) and Governor (1832–1839) of Western Australia **31** *trappings* (n) (pl): ornamental harness for a horse, including saddle, etc. • *gaily* (adv): in a joyful and happy manner **34** *mutilated* ['mju:t-] (adj): very badly damaged, esp. from cutting or tearing

1. In the first stanza the speaker describes the River Swan in Perth. What impression do you get of the river and its surroundings?
2. How are the 'end of December' (l. 14) celebrations described?
3. According to the poem, what bloody event was the river a witness to?
4. Compare and contrast 'the river's ... children' (l. 27) of past and present.
5. How is the chorus (cf. ll. 11–15, 36–40) important for the structure and the overall impact of the poem?
6. In what way do you think Jack Davis's perspective on the celebrations is shaped by his own personal history (cf. the introduction)?
7. How effective do you find a poem such as this one as a form of protest? Explain. What other forms of peaceful protest do you think can have a strong impact on a political situation?

5 Cleve's Story
Nicholas Jose

The Australian government's long programme of forcibly separating Aboriginal families is one of the most controversial chapters in the country's history (cf. the Info-Box, p. 52). Over 30 years after its official end, this sensitive period and its continued effects are today the subject of critical reports, studies, reviews, as well as films and fictional writing. In this excerpt from Nicholas Jose's novel *The Custodians* (1997), the protagonist Cleve meets his father after years of separation and learns of the events long ago which dramatically changed his life.

As they approached Wilga, after leaving the others and the truck behind at Wentworth, Joe said casually that this was the last place they had seen Cleve as a little boy. Cleve felt himself shiver. Joe said he was out picking grapes down the road at the time. Mary was at home with the kids. Joe told the story as he had heard it so many times from his wife. Cleve's story.

When the Welfare swooped all you could do was hide the kids or grab them and run, Joe said. The Welfare had the power to steal kids and make them fit into white society. The policy was to take them as young as possible before their own people could influence them.

For each of her births Mary Gordon had gone out into the bush with other women in order to avoid the hospital. She was so proud when the twins were born, Cleve and Daniel, both boys fairer than their older brother Arthur, even if other people said twins were bad luck. It was the same with her daughters. Rhonda, the first girl, was dark. Pauline, the girl who came after the twins, was the fairest of all the children. When word came that the Welfare was snooping round, it was always Pauline they worried about. Girls were the breeders. But girls could be trained into domestic servants who need never be mothers themselves.

When they saw the Welfare car coming in the dust along the road, word spread like wildfire through the settlement. 'Run, you kids, run!' Mary yelled, scooping up baby Pauline under her arm. Even the darkest child, Arthur, could not risk staying at home. The Welfare never left empty-handed.

Cleve was a smart little three-year-old. He knew where to run. He had his hiding place in the chook shed. Little Daniel was more confused. He wanted to follow Cleve, his older twin, as he did in everything else, but their mother told them always to separate if the Welfare came. Daniel ran down towards the river to the logs of fallen trees where he did when they played hide-and-seek. Rhonda and Arthur ran ahead towards the river. Mary and the baby followed in the same direction, but at a slower pace.

The Welfare car stopped and a man in a navy suit, a lady in a nurse's uniform and the driver in creased khaki shorts and long white socks stepped out. They were striding round the yard. Mary ducked behind the broad trunk of a tree and pressed against its bark. Then the baby, squeezed against its mother's heaving bosom, began to cry. The Welfare man was marching towards the river, his feet crunching the bark and leaves. Before Mary could gag the baby's mouth, the man had made a beeline for the tree. Mary was too frightened to run. The man came round behind the tree and gave a smile to discover mother and child at their game.

'Is it a boy or a girl?' he asked as he reached out calmly for the infant.

With her one strong arm, Mary held tight as the Welfare man's hands pulled the baby away. Pauline was crying her lungs out. At last, fearing the baby would be hurt, Mary let go.

'I appreciate how difficult this is for you. You're doing the best you can, but they'll have a better life with us,' the man said. 'A better chance. You must try to be a good Christian woman and understand.'

He crossed to the car with the baby and passed it over to the Welfare woman who settled in the backseat with the crying bundle in her lap. The engine was running. Cleve heard his mother's cries and was terrified. The worst had happened. All that mattered was to get Pauline back. He dashed out of the chook shed and saw the black Welfare car sputtering down the track in a cloud of dust and his mother standing in its wake, covering her face with her arm, wailing. The settlement was deserted otherwise. The little boy raced with all his might after the moving car. He drew near the car. The car was slowing. The car stopped. The car was reversing towards him.

'Cleve! Come back!' his mother shrieked from far away behind. 'Cleve! Get out of the way!'

The car door opened. Cleve thought he could dive in the open door and grab Pauline. But the man in the navy suit stepped quickly out and opened his arms wide. He seized the child. The door slammed. Cleve was kicking and squirming and punching and biting in vain. The car moved off.

He was breathing the dust of the road. He heard his mother's screams. He saw his mother fall on her knees on the track, her face covered with an arm glimpsed through the window as a car pulled away. Cleve writhed, the air filled with howling – the image locked in the back of his mind until now.

1 *Wilga*: outback station in the state of New South Wales **2** *Wentworth*: small outback town in the state of New South Wales **6** *the Welfare:* (in Australia) government officials working for the Aboriginal child welfare programme • *swoop:* (esp. of police or soldiers) visit or attack sb./sth. suddenly and without warning • *grab sb./sth.:* take or grasp sb./sth. suddenly, firmly or roughly **16** *snoop round sth.:* find out private things about sb., esp. by secretly looking around sth. (a house or other place) **21** *scoop sb./sth. up:* move or lift sb./sth. with a quick continuous movement **24** *chook* (AustE sl): chicken • *shed:* small simple building used for keeping things in **31** *creased* (adj): (of clothing) neatly pressed with a line **32** *stride:* walk with long steps • *duck behind sth.:* move your head or body behind sth. in order to avoid being hit or seen **33** *bark:* outer covering of a tree **34** *heave:* rise up and down with strong regular movements **36** *gag sb./sth.:* jn./etwas knebeln • *make a beeline for sb./sth.* (infml): go straight towards sb./sth. as quickly as you can **43** *appreciate sth.:* be fully aware of or sensitive to sth. **51** *in its wake:* im Kielwasser; (hier) in der Staubwolke **52** *wail:* protest loudly and bitterly **53** *might* (n) (fml): strength **54** *reverse:* (of a vehicle) go backwards **57** *dive in sth.:* jump through sth. (esp. an opening) with your head and arms going in first **60** *squirm:* twist about in a wriggling, snake-like motion • *in vain:* without success
63 *glimpse sb./sth.:* see sb./sth. for a moment, but not very clearly • *writhe* [raɪð]: twist or move your body without stopping, often because you are in pain

1. According to the text, what was the Welfare's motive for 'steal[ing] kids' (l. 7)?
2. Which of Mary's children were in the most danger and why?
3. What was particularly tragic about the way in which Cleve was taken?
4. How are the Welfare people presented in the text? What is your personal reaction to the way they behave?
5. Scenes like this were not uncommon in parts of Australia. How do you think such an event might affect a family? Consider both the short- and long-term consequences.
6. Imagine you were one of the three Welfare people who went to get Mary's children. When you returned to the office your boss asked you for a written report of the events, seen from your perspective. Write about 300 words.
7. Working in groups, gather further information from the Internet and other sources about the 'stolen children', the history of the government's policy and its motives. Present your results to the class.

6 To Be or Not to Be ... a Republic? Robert Hughes

In 1999, in a historic national referendum Australians voted on the question of whether their existing constitution, which recognizes the British monarch as head of state, should be kept as it is. In this excerpt from an article in the US magazine *Time* of September 25, 2000, Australian art critic Robert Hughes comments on the unusual nature of the political debate. He also offers some possible reasons for the outcome of the referendum.

It is a bizarre fact that no Australian can be the head of state of Australia. That role is reserved for the King or Queen of England, by definition a foreigner, and not even an elected foreigner: the office of the Australian head of state remains purely hereditary, open only to a small clan of Anglo-German squillionaires known as the Windsor family. This appreciably narrows the field of talent.

According to the Australian constitution – a document written for us by the English at the turn of the century – it is ultimately the English monarch who rules Australia through an unelected viceroy, the Governor-General. This official may be Australian or may not. He may, on behalf of the Queen, cancel any law enacted by the Australian government or even throw out the government and call for new elections. Or he may not. In practice he almost never does. The last and only time he did was in 1975, when the G-G, Sir John Kerr, fired the Labor government led by Gough Whitlam. This caused shock and resentment. Millions of Australians felt that Whitlam, their hero, the great reformer of government policy in the domains of race, immigration, foreign policy and the arts, had been stolen from them. There are still plenty of people around who regard this as not far from a coup d'état.

The firing of Whitlam made many Australians sit up with a jerk. It had never occured to them before that the Queen had the raw constitutional power to do such a thing. It cranked up the long-dormant impulse toward republicanism. Until the 1970s this had been an issue only for intellectuals and a few left-wing workers whose vehemence earned them an undeserved reputation as ratbags (obsessed eccentrics). The problem was democratizing the republican issue while detaching it from the ownership of the Australian left. And it did slowly broaden, though its main political instrument, the Australian Republican Movement (A.R.M.) didn't come into existence until the 1980s.

The growth of republican feeling in Australia coincided with, and was strongly encouraged by, the prime ministership (1991–96) of Paul Keating, a brilliant and abrasive Laborite much feared for his insults ('pansies' and 'unrepresentative swill' were among the milder epithets he launched at his foes in parliamentary debate) and greatly misunderstood for his tastes: given his passions for antique French clocks and Georgian furniture, Keating was the most cultivated Australian ever to serve as Prime Minister. The movement's chief unelected backer was a formidable young merchant banker named Malcolm Turnbull.

Australia's head of state,
Queen Elizabeth, with Prince Philip on
a tour of Australia in March 2000

Pro-monarchy activists in Sydney before the referendum on November 6, 1999

(Full disclosure obliges me to say that Turnbull is married to my niece Lucy, herself the deputy lord mayor of Sydney.) Despite Keating's defeat in the 1996 elections, Turnbull and his fellow republicans were able to bring the republic issue to a nationwide vote in 1999.

The result was a triumph of electoral timidity, worsened by fake populism. By a queer flip-flop of logic, a majority of Australian voters (55% to 45%) decided that to have an Australian President appointed by a democratically elected government was élitist and unsafe, whereas to have an immensely rich hereditary monarch as their head of state was somehow democratic and good. To understand how this weird inversion could occur, one must be aware that Australians are highly skeptical about the character of their 'pollies', though they have little reason to be: the level of serious political graft in Australia is extremely low.

In the end the monarchists won the referendum, not because Australians were devoted to the Queen and her successors but because feuding republicans couldn't agree on which model of republic to uphold. Should the new-style head of state, an Australian President, be appointed by Parliament? Or elected in a national campaign, in the American manner? The A.R.M. wanted the former, but Australians hated the idea of an American-style republic – or American-style anything – in their public life. This split the republican vote, to the boundless relief of the monarchists, who could never have carried the issue on their own. (Pollsters thought that about 70% of Australians were for a republic of some kind.) [...]

It is hard to say why, apart from habit, there should be any nostalgia for royal forms among Australians, especially when we are so fond of our national antiélitism. But people, including Australians, want figures to admire. 'If we don't have the Queen, whom can we look up to?' was one of the most frequent complaints at referendum time. The thought that in a democracy you don't look up to your superiors, but sideways at your fellow citizens, wasn't much aired in monarchist circles. And Australia has always been short not only of convincing shared ceremonies of national identity but also of shared folk heroes. [...]

Another reason why some Australians want to keep the monarchy is unease about mixture. The Queen evokes the loyalty and gratitude of the 'pure' Anglo-Australian because she personifies 'pure' Britain. This worked fine a half-century ago, when more than 90% of Australians were still of British descent and could feel themselves to be, as Prime Minister Robert Menzies would later put it, 'British to the bootheels'. But today the picture of exclusionary Australia, the continent-size British island just below Asia, has almost faded away. The White Australia Policy, that disgraceful provision whereby no one of Asian or black descent could settle in Australia, was abandoned in the 1960s, never to be revived. Whole suburbs, like Cabramatta in western Sydney, have become Southeast Asian enclaves. Though Australia admits only some 85,000 legal immigrants a year, a miniscule fraction of its population, the Asian component, is very visible and it excites xenophobia. The role of the Queen as head of state has a calming effect, suggesting that the 'old' Anglo-Australia is still notionally within reach.

6 *hereditary* [-'- - - -]: legally given to sb.'s child when that person dies **7** *squillionnaire* (non-standard): immensely rich person whose wealth cannot be measured **8** *Windsor family:* British royal family since 1917 • *appreciable* (adj): beträchtlich, erheblich **12** *ultimately* (adv): in the end, finally **14** *viceroy:* person who is sent by a king or queen to govern a country **16** *cancel sth.:* etwas rückgängig machen • *enact sth.:* make sth. (esp. a proposal) into law **23** *resentment:* Ärger, Groll **25** *domain:* area of activity, concern, or function **29** *coup d'etat* [ˌkuː deɪ'tɑː] (French): sudden overthrow of a government **31** *jerk:* sudden abrupt motion

33–34 *crank sth. up* (infml): make a machine, etc., work or work at a higher level **40** *detach sth. from sth.:* separate sth. from sth. **47** *coincide with sth.* [ˌkəʊɪn'saɪd]: (of two or more events) take place at the same time as sth. **49** *abrasive* [ə'breɪsɪv]: seeming rude or unkind because you say what you think very directly **50** *pansy* (n) (derog): offensive word for a man who seems weak and too much like a woman **51** *swill* (n): mixture of waste food and water that is given to pigs to eat; (here) rubbish **52** *epithet:* (in the USA) offensive word or phrase that is used about a person or group • *foe* (fml): enemy **55** *Georgian:* relating to, or characteristic of the period in which the four kings ruled Great Britain and Ireland from 1714 to 1830 **58** *formidable:* earning respect because sb./sth. is powerful or impressive **60** *disclosure* (n) (fml): act of making sth. known or public that was secret or private before **66** *timidity* (n): condition of being fearful and lacking confidence **67** *fake:* not real or authentic • *flip-flop* (n): change or switch, esp. to the exact opposite position **74** *weird* [wɪəd]: strange, not normal **77** *pollie* (AustE infml): politician **79** *graft* (n): use of illegal or unfair methods to gain advantage in business, politics, etc. **83** *feud* [fjuːd]: have an angry and bitter argument with sb. over a long period of time **91** *split sth.:* divide sth.

93 *pollster:* person who makes or asks the questions in an opinion poll (= Umfrage) **98** *be fond of sth.:* find sth. pleasant or enjoyable, esp. sth. you have liked for a long time **112** *evoke sth.:* bring sth. (esp. a feeling, image or memory) into your mind **124–125** *abandon sb./sth.:* give up sb./sth. **129** *miniscule:* very small, tiny

131 *xenophobia* [ˌzenə-]: strong feeling of dislike or fear of people from other countries

134 *notional* (adj): speculative or theoretical

1. According to Robert Hughes, what event in 1975 do many Australians feel was 'not far from a coup d'état' (ll. 28–29) and why?
2. Why does Hughes view the outcome of the referendum in 1999 as a 'weird inversion' (ll. 74–75)?
3. According to the writer, why do some Australians still prefer to have the British monarch as their head of state?
4. Describe the writer's personal view. List the words and passages from the text which support your conclusion.
5. Hughes states that '... Australia has always been short not only of convincing shared ceremonies of national identity but also of shared folk heroes' (ll. 106–109). In your opinion, how important are 'ceremonies of national identity' and national folk heroes? Consider examples of each from your own country.

Youth, Lifestyle and Culture

1 Backyard John Tranter

John Tranter, a leading figure in Australian poetry, often writes about the uglier side of modern life with all its weaknesses and failures. His poems tell of lives filled with anger, greed, passion, and lost in the illusions of a complex, material world. A typical suburban home and a popular Australian pastime provide the setting for 'Backyard', a poem from Tranter's collection *Under Berlin: New Poems* (1988).

The God of Smoke listens idly in the heat
to the barbecue sausages
speaking the language of rain deceitfully
as their fat dances.

Azure, hazed, the huge drifting sky shelters
its threatening weather.
A screen door slams, and the kids come tumbling
out of their arguments,

and the barrage of shouting begins, concerning
young Sandra and Scott
and the broken badminton racquet and net
and the burning meat.

1 *idle* [aɪdl] (adj): lazy, not working hard **3** *deceitful* [dɪˈsiːtfl] (adj): behaving in a dishonest way **5** *azure* [ˈæʒə]: bright blue in colour like the sky • *hazed* (adj): (of air) difficult to see through because of smoke, dust or moisture **7** *screen door:* door which has a framed wire or plastic mesh, used to keep out insects and permit the flow of air • *tumble:* fall or roll end over end **9** *barrage of sth.* [ˈbærɑːʒ ☆ bəˈrɑːʒ]: large number of sth. (e.g. questions or comments) that are directed at sb. very quickly, one after the other, esp. in an aggressive way **14** *heavens:* (spoken) used to show that you are surprised or annoyed **17** *worry sth.:* (of a dog) attack sth. (esp. another animal) by chasing or biting it; (here) dig up sth. (the grass) **21** *tattered* (adj): old and torn; in bad condition **22–23** *rite of passage:* ceremony performed in some cultures at times when a person changes their status, e.g. at puberty and marriage **23** *adolescence* [- - ˈ- -]: transitional period of life between youth and adulthood **28** *Southerly Buster* [ˈsʌðəli] (in Australia) strong ocean wind in the coastal region around Sydney which comes from the south, usually in the evenings following very hot days

Is that a fifties home movie, or the real
thing? Heavens, how
a child and a beach ball in natural colour
can break your heart.

And the brown dog worries the khaki grass
to stop it from growing
in place of his worship, the burying bone.
The bone that stinks.

Turn now to the God of this tattered arena
watching over the rites
of passage – marriage, separation; adolescence
and troubled maturity:

having served under that bright sky you may look up
but don't ask too much:
some cold beer, a few old friends in the afternoon,
a Southerly Buster at dusk.

1. What is your immediate feeling after reading the poem? Compare your reaction with those of others in your class.
2. Two gods are mentioned in the poem (cf. ll. 1, 21). What does each appear to be responsible for?
3. How are the children, 'young Sandra and Scott' (l. 10) represented in the poem?
4. How do the 'rites of passage' (ll. 22–23) contrast with the homely backyard scene which the speaker describes?
5. Why does the speaker refer to the backyard scene as 'this tattered arena' (l. 21)? How does this reflect his attitude?
6. Tranter's poem is set in his native Australia. To what extent do you think non-Australian readers can identify with the poem?

2 The Options Generation

Sophie Tedmanson

Here Sophie Tedmanson investigates the attitudes and perspectives of young people down under: how they see themselves and their generation, what influences them most, and what their future might hold. The text is taken from a special report in the magazine *Weekend Australian* of January 3–4, 1998.

Surfers are hanging out on Sydney beaches, ravers are dancing to techno music at a rave party in the Adelaide Hills, indie kids are rocking on at a gig at The Loft in Perth, goths are going underground in Melbourne, and in Darwin a scrum of under-20 rugby players are drinking rounds of VB at The Vic on the mall. [...]

It's youth culture, and it involves every young person. But what was a way of life to the previous generation is now simply a way of living. Young people are rebelling against the group culture ethic and announcing themselves as individuals. Individuals, that is, who still feel the need to belong.

Sound confusing? Try asking any young person what they think of youth culture and they'll look you in the eye and tell you they are an individual. That they don't 'need to belong' to any particular group. Such urban stereotyping, they say, makes them angry.

The 'options' or 'hang loose' generation is what social researcher and commentator Hugh Mackay calls them. They are a generation which defies generalisation, he says, which wants to be seen as highly individualistic and independent.

'Part of the contradiction is that they are actually a very dependent generation,' he says. 'They stay at home longer, they stay at school longer, they go onto the dole sooner and in larger numbers. But they see themselves as independent and certainly as individuals, which is why they tend not to lock into one particular sub-culture in a permanent way.'

Pierre Toussaint agrees with the 'options' tag. The 24-year-old editor of Soup, a Perth pop-culture street magazine, believes today's youth have too many options, which lead them down the path of confusion. Many, for example, study various courses at uni, then change their minds again upon graduation.

The fear of commitment, says Mackay, whether to a partner, political party, course, job or religious belief, stems from growing up in a rapidly changing world. Today's youth is forced to deal with issues far removed from those of their parents' generation.

They have been raised in a society of huge social, cultural, economic and technological changes – they were taught to beware of strangers in kindergarten, had AIDS education in primary school, are often faced with drugs and violence in high school. They are street smart and comprehensive. Yet, says Mackay, the constant craving for 'the next thing' creates insecurities. 'Combined with massive insecurities of the job market and the insecurities associated with the fact that they are the offspring of our most divorced ever generation – that's what causes there to be such a strong drive for a youth culture which gives these people a sense of identity.'

It's not permanence, he says, but a sense of identity along the way. 'It's a fairly rapidly changing thing. Short fashion cycles and a reluctance to commit to being part of one culture reflects the kaleidoscopic world and how things are changing so rapidly.'

[...]

Lin and Sari, both 22-year-old stall-holders at Sydney's Glebe flea-markets, a hub of youth culture and a kind of alternative supermarket, believe young people identify with cultures as a way of 'searching desperately to find a personality'. Yet youth culture is so diverse that it's difficult to do something different and actually be an individual. They also agree that young people feel the need to belong because of the breakdown of the family unit. 'I don't think the family (influence) on youth culture is very stressed,' Lin says. 'There's no sense of unity (in families) – with youth culture, there is a need to feel wanted and of belonging.'

The director of learning and teaching at Charles Stuart University, Dr Mark McFadden, studied a group of street kids looking for access to tertiary education and found the most common thread was that they all came from broken families. 'If young people don't fit in with their family and don't fit into their school, they look for a group they can fit in with to get a sense of belonging,' he says. 'They therefore get involved with and are influenced by the kinds of practises that group believes are important. The kids I was dealing with were not typical of average kids, but they represent a growing number of the student population.'

Surprisingly, he says given their background, the youths were optimistic about their future, believing education was the key to success. Surveys published recently in The Medical Journal of Australia found most young people think the opposite. They showed young people were more mistrustful, cynical and pessimistic about the future than the generations preceding them.

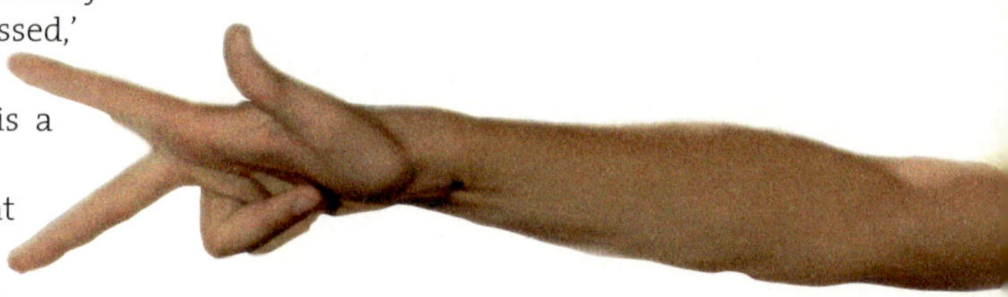

1. What does Tedmanson mean when she describes the youth culture of the previous generation as a 'way of life' (l. 9) and the present-day youth culture as a 'way of living' (ll. 10–11)?
2. Why does Hugh Mackay call young Australians today the 'options generation' (l. 21)? What contradiction does he see in this?
3. What insecurities are today's teenagers faced with? How, according to the text, do they react to these insecurities?
4. Australian writer Mark Davis states that in the West we have 'a very strong culture of the individual that everyone aspires to, but it's a bit mythological'. Write a comment on this view based on your own personal experience.
5. What similarities and differences do you see between young people in Australia as described in the text and young people in your country? Explain and discuss in class.

1 *hang out* (infml): spend a lot of (free) time in a place **3** *indie* (adj): used to describe popular music played by bands that are new and not well known, that is produced by small independent companies **4** *gig* (n): performance by musicians playing pop music or jazz in front of an audience • *goth* (n): member of a group of people who wear black clothes and black and white make-up and listen to goth music, a style of rock music with words often expressing dark ideas about death, the devil or the end of the world **6** *scrum* (n): (of rugby) part of the game when players from both teams interlock heads and shoulders and push against each other; the ball is then thrown in between them and each side tries to get it; (here) group **7** *VB:* brand of Australian beer • *mall = shopping mall:* large group of shops/stores built together under one roof and closed to traffic **14** *belong:* feel comfortable and happy with a particular group of people **24** *defy sb./sth.:* resist sb./sth. **30** *go on to the dole* (BE infml): receive unemployment money from the state **35** *tag* (infml): description, name **41** *graduation:* act of successfully completing secondary school or university studies **42** *commitment:* promise to do sth. or behave in a certain way **44** *stem from sth.:* be the result of sth. **55** *craving* (n): strong desire for sth. **59** *offspring* (fml): child/children of a particular person or animal • *divorced* (adj): geschieden **61** *drive for sth.:* effort by a group of people to achieve sth. **66** *reluctance:* unwillingness **68** *kaleidoscopic* (adj): containing different parts that are constantly changing **93** *tertiary* ['tɜːʃəri ☆ -ʃieri] (adj): (of education) university or college level **94** *thread* [θred]: idea or feature which connects the different parts of sth. **95** *broken family:* family in which the mother and father have divorced **104** *given:* angesichts

3 Olympics Gave Indigenous Australians Their Biggest Ever Stage

Mike Corder

Despite negative predictions, the Olympics Games in Sydney in August 2000 were an integrating event for multicultural Australia. One particular athlete played a central role, as an Australian and as an Aborigine, while the cultural programme drew attention to Aboriginal issues. The powerful mixture of sport, culture and politics at these Games is the subject of this article from London's *Independent* of October 2, 2000.

Aboriginal myths at the opening ceremony. Cathy Freeman lighting the cauldron and blazing to victory in the 400 meters race. Indigenous rock group Yothu Yindi's closing ceremony performance. From start to finish, the Sydney Olympics provided indigenous Australians with their biggest ever stage and they used it to create lasting, positive images of one of the world's oldest cultures. Ahead of Sydney 2000, there were threats that Aborigines seeking to highlight decades of marginalization, neglect and abuse would disrupt the games.

Instead, they enriched them.

'I guess it shows there were a lot of people very supportive of Aboriginal issues, and want to make sure that Aboriginal culture is showcased to the world,' Gary Ella, head of the games organising committee's indigenous program, said Monday. 'It comes to the stage now where some people have to make some decisions ... and continue to take the reconciliation process forward.'

Angry at the faltering process toward reconciliation between Australia's black and white communities, prominent activist Charles Perkins predicted before the games that Abori-

Left: The opening ceremony of the Sydney Olympics

Right: Cathy Freeman's gold-medal performance was a momentous occasion for Australians of all backgrounds.

gines would riot, torching cars and houses to protest their status as Australia's most underprivileged people. But anger was defused from the first beat of the opening ceremony, which was steeped in indigenous imagery, and the choice of Freeman, an Aborigine, to light the cauldron. Freeman's rousing victory in the 400 meters was another defining moment for Australia – black and white.

'She's brought the people of Australia together as one group,' said Bruce Barber, Freeman's stepfather. 'Whether it is Anglo Saxon, Asian or whatever, she's admired by so many people.' Sir Gustav Nossal, chairman of the government–funded National Reconciliation Council, said the Olympics did more in two weeks to promote reconciliation than governments have achieved in years. 'You could not have had a better deal for reconciliation than these Olympics have been,' he told ABC radio. 'I think the world will recognize that there is a journey of healing – that the Australian people as a whole want reconciliation.' Indigenous themes continued through to Sunday night's closing party, with rock band Midnight Oil wearing black clothes emblazoned with the word 'sorry'. Aborigines want a national apology for their past mistreatment but Prime Minister John Howard has refused. Yothu Yindi, Australia's best-known Aboriginal musicians, played their anthemic hit 'Treaty', calling for a treaty between white Australia and Aborigines setting out indigenous rights.

Australia's original inhabitants, Aborigines number about 360,000 of a total population of 19 million people. Aborigines have a life expectancy 20 years shorter than the rest of society and are the community's poorest, least educated and most jailed people.

Ella predicted the reconciliation process would be pushed along by the Olympics. The games were 'one of those great events that no one could turn a blind eye to,' he told ABC television. Howard, whose refusal to apologise has angered many indigenous and white Australians, agreed. 'We will continue to have debate about these things but I do think (there is a) sense of cohesion and exhilaration that people felt during these games,' he told ABC radio. 'There we were, represented by a team that was, I suppose, redolent of every strand in Australian society – different ethnic backgrounds, Aboriginal and other different backgrounds. I think it just demonstrated what a cohesive country we were and that doesn't alter the fact that you are going to have debates about whether you should have formal apologies.'

1. **According to the article, what speculations were voiced before the Olympics and why did these speculations not come true (cf. ll. 9–19, 29–35)?**
2. **What did Sir Gustav Nossal mean when he spoke of Australia's 'journey of healing' (l. 48)?**
3. **According to the text, what role have the Sydney Olympics played in relations between indigenous and non-indigenous Australians?**
4. **Many people feel that the Olympic Games should never be used as an international platform for expressing political views. To what extent do you agree or disagree with this view and why?**
5. **Find examples from history in which political issues have had a less positive influence on the Olympic Games. Discuss your results.**

2 *cauldron* ['kɔːldrən ☆ 'kaːl-]: large deep pot used for cooking things over a fire; here, the large round structure containing the Olympic flame **11** *marginalization:* act of making a group of people unimportant and powerless **12** *neglect* (n): fact of not giving enough care or attention to sth./sb. • *abuse* [ə'bjuːs] (n): unfair, cruel or violent treatment of sb. **13** *enrich sth.:* improve the quality of sth. **16–17** *showcase sb./sth.:* display sb./sth. prominently, esp. in an attractive way **21** *reconciliation* [ˌrekənsɪli'eɪʃn]: settling or resolving of a problem or disagreement so that a good relationship can exist again **23** *falter:* become weaker or less effective **27** *riot* ['raɪət] (v): (of a crowd of people) behave in a violent way in a public place, often in protest **29** *defuse sth.* [diː'fjuːz]: stop sth. (a dangerous or difficult situation) from developing, esp. by making people less angry or nervous **31** *be steeped in sth.:* have a lot of sth. (esp. a particular quality) **46** *ABC* (abbr.) = *Australian Broadcasting Corporation:* Australian public television and radio organization
51–52 *Midnight Oil:* popular Australian pop group **52** *emblazon sth. with sth.* [ɪm'bleɪzn]: decorate sth. with sth. (esp. a sign, a symbol or words so that people will notice it easily)
57 *anthemic* (nonstandard): (of a song) having special importance for a country or group and played at special occasions • *treaty:* Vertrag
62–63 *life expectancy:* Lebenserwartung
69 *turn a blind eye to sth.:* ignore sth.
74 *cohesion* [kəʊ'hiːʒn] (fml): act or state of sticking together; tendency to unite **77** *redolent of sth.* (adj): making you think of sth.

$$n = \frac{V}{V_m} \quad n = \frac{V_n}{V_{m,n}}$$

$$C = \varepsilon_0 \cdot \varepsilon_r \cdot \frac{A}{s} = \varepsilon \cdot \frac{A}{s}$$

$$M(B) = k_S \cdot \frac{m(B)}{\Delta T_S \cdot m(Lm)}$$

$$s = \sqrt{s^2} = \sqrt{\sum_{i=1}^{k} (x_i - \bar{x})^2 \cdot h_n(x_i)}$$

$$F = N_A \cdot e$$

4 Education: Our New Great Divide

Do private schools produce better students? If so, why? The following editorial from Melbourne's *The Age* of June 7, 1998, is a comment on the different opportunities which students in private and public schools face and the long-term advantages and shortcomings of Australia's dual system of education.

There are not twice as many clever children at private schools as there are at state schools, but more than twice as many private-school students go on to university. Why is this? There are many reasons attendance at a private school has always given students a better chance of going to university, and most of them have to do with inequality of opportunity. It is disappointing though that – despite new equity programs, despite far more state school students completing the final year of secondary education, and despite a huge increase in tertiary enrolments across the board – still only 30 per cent of state-school students attend universities compared with 72 per cent of private-school students.

Undoubtedly, parental occupation, income and attitudes to education, academic ability and ethnic background influence whether a student enrols in higher education, but the biggest influence, as a recent study by the Australian Council for Education Research shows, is the type of school attended. And since there is considerable inequality between schools, it is scarcely surprising that this is reflected in university enrolments. As private-school students interviewed in *The Age* last week pointed out, private schools can offer students more options, better resources and more individual tuition to help them get the marks they need to get into university. Private schools also have the option, unlike state schools, of rejecting students they consider to have insufficient academic ability.

Australia's dual system of education, despite periodic calls for the ending of state aid to private schools, has served it well. But taxpayer support of private schools should not be at the expense of the state system, which still educates 70 per cent of children. During the Howard Government's first term of office, government support for private schools has increased considerably at some expense to the state school system, and a user-pays approach to university education has been intensified. In Victoria, deep cuts to education and a reliance on 'voluntary' school levies is in danger of creating a two-tier system even within the state school system.

Australia is a wealthy enough society to ensure that all children, not only the children of the rich, are educated to the best of their ability. A clever country needs to maximise the intellectual assets of all its citizens, not just those who enjoy the privileges of monetary wealth.

5 *attendance:* act of being present at a place, e.g. at school **9** *despite* (prep): trotz • *equity* (n) (fml): situation in which everyone is treated fairly **12** *increase in sth.* (n): rise in the amount, number or value of sth. • *tertiary* (adj): (of education) university or college level **13** *enrolment* (BE) = (AE) *enrollment*: act of officially joining a course, school, etc. • *across the board:* allgemein, generell **25** *scarcely* ['skeəsli] (adv): kaum **29** *resource* (n): something that can be used to help achieve an aim, esp. a book, equipment, etc. **30** *tuition* [tju'ɪʃn ☆ tu-] (fml): act of teaching sth., esp. to one person or to small groups **33** *insufficient* (fml): inadequate **38–39** *at the expense of sth.:* auf Kosten einer Sache **41** *Howard Government:* government of Prime Minister John Howard (1996–1998, 1998–2001, 2001–present) **44** *user-pays approach:* (here) policy whereby students pay university enrolment fees themselves (fees in Australia were previously paid by the government)
45 *Victoria:* state in south-eastern Australia whose capital city is Melbourne **47** *levy* ['levi]: extra amount of money that has to be paid • *two-tier:* zweigestuft **53** *asset* ['- -]: person or thing that is valuable or useful to sb./sth.

1. What main reason is given for the fact that, compared to state schools, 'more than twice as many private-school students go on to university' (ll. 3–4)?
2. What advantages do private schools have over state schools?
3. What basic problem with Australia's dual system of education does this editorial point to?
4. Explain the title of the editorial and the reference which it makes. You may need to consult a dictionary, an encyclopeadia or online sources.
5. What technique does the writer use to start and finish his or her commentary (cf. ll. 1–4, 52–54) and what is its effect?
6. Germany has a very low percentage of private schools (2%) compared to Australia (30%). Discuss in groups what advantages and disadvantages an increase in their numbers might possibly bring in Germany.
7. Imagine you had to decide whether to send your children to a public (state) or private school. Which would you choose? Explain your answer.

5 Strine George Mikes

Australians are particularly known and loved for their unique variety of English, a way of speaking which reflects their informal and easy-going attitude to most things. In this text Hungarian-born English writer George Mikes clears up some favourite misconceptions about this colourful dialect and its users.

When it comes to language, Australians are somewhat resentful or at least silent, about something they should be proud of; and are proud of something about which they might as well remain silent.

Should someone remark that the Australian language, Strine – that's what it sounds like when an Aussie says 'Australian' – is closely related to cockney, Australians are deeply offended. Cockneys, it is true, are even more deeply offended. This mutual touchiness, however, does not alter the truth. Most of the convicts, warders and other early arrivals, who laid the foundations of Australian speech, came from the London area and Essex. There were others, of course, but the London-Essex group was predominant and absorbed the linguistic impact of the others. Welsh, too, had a noticeable influence on Strine for a time but these traces subsequently disappeared. [...]

Cockney may not be beautiful, but it is rich, humorous, original and vigorous. Australia has every reason to be satisfied with her linguistic parentage.

Where misplaced pride comes into play, is where Australia's original contribution to the language is concerned. This is regarded as immense; in fact, it is neither immense nor infinitesimal: it is average. Australians show neither more nor less resourcefulness in inventing words and phrases than most other nations. I am only emphasizing this because there is a legend to the contrary. A well-educated gentleman seriously informed me that Australia had a genius for slang and that Australians had enriched the English language by 500,000 original words. Considering that the larger Oxford Dictionary contains 470,000 words altogether, this is quite a claim. (The number of genuine Australian words is estimated by experts at between 1,500 and 2,000.)

Many of these original words are Aboriginal words; quite a few are survivals from the settler days. Words like *jimbangs* and *sollicker* sound magnificent, but the truth is that a considerable proportion of these most exotic words come from that faraway and exotic land, called Britain. *Sollicker* (meaning force) is derived from Yorkshire; *mudfat* from Northern Ireland; *mullock* is recorded in English dialect vocabularies; and to *fossick* (to search) is Cornish. Of the many Aboriginal words, *gilgai*, *boomerang*, *woomera*, *kangaroo*, *wallaby*, *potoroo*, *kookaburra* and *billabong* are just a very few. The desire to live in a town called Wagga Wagga or in a suburb called Woolloomooloo has, on occasions, an almost irresistible fascination for me. *Billabong*, by the way, is the second most popular Australian word. The only trouble with it is that no one really knows what it means. Mr Ramson admits in his book (not in so many words) that he has no idea. The *most* popular Australian word is *dinkum*. 'Fair dinkum' (meaning 'Oh, really?') is reported to be the most often used and most truly Australian phrase. I heard it used only and exclusively by New Australians of short standing who wanted to prove what fine Aussies they had become in no time.

That was a hard yakker!

To call a Tasmanian a Tassie, an Australian an Aussie and football footy, is not sparklingly witty. Some phrases are better; others again are very good. The country is the bush and outlaws were the bushrangers; the bush telegraph is the grapevine, the bush lawyer is the man who thinks he is proficient in law, and bush-language is, in fact, not half as obscene as one would imagine. To bush is also a verb; if you get bushed in a big city, you've lost your way. 'She's apples' means that she's all right, quite reliable. If someone goes crook on you, he or she is angry with you or persecutes you. To have a dekko is to have a look out and when you come a gutzer your carefully laid plans fall through. A jackeroo is an apprentice at a sheep-station and if you go home very late, your wife may turn lemony on you. A bird is a sheila and a tough job is a hard yakker. But as I said, no one knows what a billabong is.[1] The trouble is that the best and most original Australian slang is robustly obscene and therefore, alas, unprintable.[2]

I tried to find out what impact New Australians had made on the language, but all the authorities maintain that it is nil or almost nil. This lack of impact is mutual. New Australians made no impact on English; and English made no impact on many New Australians.

A few months ago, two of my ex-Hungarian friends – now living in Australia and full members of the HWC[3] – visited me in London. I drove them around in the country and took them, one day, to the Cotswolds. They went

Have a dekko at this...

into a village newsagent's to buy cigarettes and picture-postcards and as they seemed to be taking a very long time, I went in after them. The newsagent turned to me and asked:

'You're Australian too?'

'What makes you think so?' I asked.

'You have the same accent as the two other gentlemen.'

2 *resentful* (adj): feeling of anger or unhappiness about sth. that you think is unfair **7** *cockney:* person from the East End of London; way of speaking that is typical of cockneys • *offend sb.* [- ˈ-]: make sb. angry or upset **8** *mutual* [ˈmjuːtʃuəl] (adj): shared by two or more people • *touchiness* (infml): sensitivity • *alter:* ändern **9** *convict* [ˈkɒn- ☆ ˈkɑːn-]: person who has been found guilty of a crime and sent to prison • *warder* (BE): prison guard **10** *Essex:* county in south-eastern England **13** *trace:* mark, object or sign that shows that sth. existed or was present **13** *subsequent* (adj): happening after sth. else **17** *misplaced* (adj): not appropriate or correct in the situation **19** *infinitesimal* (fml): extremely small **20** *resourcefulness:* quality of being good at finding ways of doing things and solving problems, etc. **21** *emphasize sth.:* etwas betonen **25** *claim* (n): Behauptung **20** *jimbang* (AustE sl): lot, concern, affair (e.g. 'the whole lot') **32** *mudfat* (AustE sl): as fat as possible **33** *mullock* (AustE sl) (n): rubbish **36** *Wagga Wagga:* township in the state of Queensland **37** *Woolloomooloo*: suburb of Sydney, New South Wales • *irresistible* [ˌ- - ˈ- - -]: unwiderstehlich **39** *Mr Ramson = W. S. Ramson:* Australian linguist and author of *Australian English* (1966) **41** *dinkum* (AustE sl): real/genuine, right **43** *standing* (n): social or professional position of sb./sth. in relation to others **46** *sparkling* (adj): brilliant **48** *grapevine* (infml): unofficial way of passing on information, esp. from person to person **49** *proficient* [prəˈfɪʃnt]: able to do sth. well or skilfully **51** *reliable* [riˈlaɪəbl]: zuverlässig **52** *persecute sb.:* treat sb. in a cruel or unfair way **55** *bird* (BE infml): woman **58** *alas* [əˈlæs] (old use): exclamation used to show you are sad or sorry **59** *impact:* effect **65** *the Cotswolds*: range of low scenic hills in south-western England

[1] Stop press news: a billabong is a waterhole
[2] Some of the above examples are taken from *Aussie English* by John O'Grady (Nino Culotta), Ure Smith, 1965; some others from W.S. Ramson's book and a modest two or three come from my own collection.
[3] Hungarian World Conspiracy

She's a dinkum Tassie.

1. According to Mikes, what are Australians 'deeply offended' (l. 7) about? Why, in his view, should they not be offended?
2. According to the writer, what are the two main origins of many 'Australian' words (cf. ll. 28–31)?
3. What does the author try to show when he describes his experience in the Cotswolds in England (cf. ll. 63–71)?
4. Describe the tone of the text and give examples to illustrate.
5. Slang is common in most cultures. In your experience, in what sorts of situations do people often use slang and why? Discuss.
6. In the Internet you can find numerous dictionaries of Australian English. Working in pairs, choose seven Australian slang terms from one of these dictionaries and compose a short text (about 250 words) using the terms. Exchange your text with others in your class and see how quickly you can 'decode' their text.

6 Art of the Dreaming

Visual art in Aboriginal culture takes a number of different forms, among them painting, wood carving and weaving. Most of this richly symbolic work can only be fully understood and appreciated in the context of indigenous culture. The following text explores the background to Aboriginal art. It also talks about how indigenous artists and artisans have responded to the growing interest in their work in and outside of Australia.

Traditional religious art

Like Aboriginal oral history, the visual arts illustrate and record a monumental timespan. Over 40,000 years, Aborigines expressed their intellectual and religious attitudes to the land and the meaning of life through elaborate art and ceremony.

A rich oral mythology expressed in ceremonial life is at the very centre of Aboriginal culture. Essentially, all tribal groups believe that their ancestral spirits entered Australia in the creation time, or the Dreaming, when the landscape was partly formed. Some, such as the giant serpents, came from beneath the ground. As they moved, they created ridges and valleys and behind them rivers flowed into the sea. Many Aborigines also believe that the creation ancestors filled and fashioned the cosmos, becoming the sun, moon, stars and planets.

Each clan claimed tracts of land by virtue of descent from the spiritual ancestors. Certain people had the duty of guarding sacred sites, visiting and retouching art, conducting ceremonies at special places, or clearing unwanted vegetation from sacred rocks and trees.

The exceptionally strong relationship with ancestral heroes and with the landscape forms the basis of all Aboriginal art. Dance, song, ceremony and material arts all combine to form a unified whole, a complete artistic network that articulates the landscape and the Dreaming.

Symbolism

Representational art showing human and animal forms exists beside abstract symbols. Essentially, the symbols can be used for a number of purposes, and members of different groups understand each other's symbols to varying degrees.

The Walpiri-Pintubi communities of the western desert region create magnificent ground designs from plant down, ochre and clay. These are patterns showing the land, as well as events of the creation era. A range of symbols is used, including arcs, concentric circles, circles, bars, dots and wavy lines. The meaning of the symbols varies in every painting, depending on the site shown, the religious inferences, the degree of information the authors have been allowed to convey (their ritual status) and the status of the intended audience.

In a sense, some of the symbols can be used like an alphabet but when put together they create a meaning that is totally accessible only to the creators of their immediate group.

When symbols are used together to form a ground plan of a design, they map the landscape showing special features with important mythological relevance to the subject matter depicted. They also tell stories about events in the Dreaming. Their reproducing the designs becomes a religious act of reaffirmation of belief in the creation ancestors and the absorption of their essential power.

Arnhem Land painting has a symbolic visual language distinctly different from that of other areas of eastern Arnhem Land, each clan owns a wide range of patterns and designs that signify areas of land, natural features or specific objects. Representational figures of men, animals, fish and plants are incorporated into art, but a full interpretation depends on the pattern and designs used in relation to the figurative elements.

The giant carved trees, or dendroglyphs, of the southeast were made to mark initiation grounds and burial sites. The patterns of spirals, lozenges and zigzags denote territorial ownership. Ceremonies and trading visits between Aboriginal tribes were announced by messengers sent from one to the other. So that the messages would be received at their destination, messengers were given message sticks incised with symbols and patterns – which would allow them to pass unmolested through strange country. The patterns not only identified the carrier by symbolising his territory, but, in some instances, they conveyed the message itself.

Symbols and signs continue to be part of traditional Aboriginal communication. Stones are left in patterns of tracks, and circles and lines are drawn in the sand as an aid to conversation and storytelling. [...]

Marketing of Aboriginal art

Within the last decade Aboriginal art has become an important aspect of the economy of remote communities. Women produce bark paintings or carvings as well as a range of woven baskets, string bags and conical dillybags. The surfaces of women's softwood carvings at Yirrkala are finely gouged in the manner of wood blocks, then painted in natural ochres. Men, in keeping with the traditional division of the sexes, concentrate on men's weapons and bark paintings.

There is considerable demand for Aboriginal traditional art within Australia and an increasing number of international exhibitions. The artworks are purchased by community-based art advisers. They are then transported to community centres of which there are now over 100.

Each centre follows the locally based policy of directly exhibiting the work in southern states in private galleries or selling paintings on a wholesale basis. Aboriginal art has attracted the interest of major art collectors and is now represented in all Australian galleries and an increasing number of important international contemporary art collections.

In the desert areas the interest in modern acrylic paintings has produced an explosion of talent. Many artists also work independently in towns of the outback, particularly Alice Springs, in the Northern Territory, where tourism is an important component of the local economy.

Modern Aboriginal art includes painting, print-making, contemporary crafts, ceramics and fabric printing. Urban artists have formed art cooperatives. Many of these artists have received formal art school education and their works, although diverse in style, reflect the urgent social and political considerations of Aborigines today.

Boomalli Aboriginal Artists' Co-operative in Sydney is one such focus for urban artists. An important issue facing all traditional artists is copyright of their designs and their use in Australia and elsewhere. Although the art is made for sale, traditional art is religious and is considered the exclusive copyright not only of the individual but of the clan or group as well.

There is, in a sense, an unspoken understanding on the part of the artists that the buyers will act as responsible custodians of the paintings.

2 *oral:* transmitted by words **4** *attitude:* Einstellung, Haltung **5** *elaborate* [ɪ'læbərət] (adj): complex and rich in detail **7** *ancestral:* relating to a person or persons in your family who lived long ago **9** *serpent:* large snake **10** *ridge* [rɪdʒ]: narrow area of high land along the top of a line of hills or mountains **12** *fashion sth.:* give sth. shape or form **14** *tract:* Gebiet • *by virtue of:* on the grounds or basis of • *descent from sb.* [dɪ'sent]: person's family origins **15** *sacred* ['seɪkrɪd] (adj): connected with a god or religion **16** *retouch sth.* (v): make small changes to sth. (esp. a picture or photograph) so that it looks better **23** *representational:* (of a style of art or painting) trying to show things as they really are **26** *degree:* amount or level of sth. **28** *down* (n): Daunen **29** *pattern:* Muster • *range:* variety **30** *arc:* part of a circle or a curved line **32** *inference* ['ɪnfərəns]: sth. that you can find out indirectly from what you already know
33 *convey sth.:* communicate or make sth. known **36** *accessible:* easy to understand
37 *immediate* [ɪ'mi:diət]: next to or very close to a particular place or time **45** *depict sth.:* represent sth. in a picture **51** *reaffirmation* [ˌri:æfə'meɪʃn] (fml): repeated statement of sth. in order to emphasize that it is still true **52** *absorption:* (here) act of taking sth. (a special power) into oneself
53 *Arnhem Land:* region in Australia's Northern Territory (cf. the map, inside cover) **57** *incorporate sth. into sth.:* include sth. so that it forms a part of sth. **60** *initiation* [ɪ'nɪʃi'eɪʃn]: act of sb. becoming a member of a group, often with a special ceremony • *lozenge* ['lɒzɪndʒ ☆ 'lɑ:z-]: four-sided figure in the shape of a diamond
61 *denote sth.* (fml): mean or represent sth.
64 *incise sth.:* cut into sth., as with a sharp instrument **65** *unmolested* (adj): not disturbed or attacked by sb.; not prevented from doing sth. **73** *bark:* outer covering of a tree **74** *conical:* kegelförmig • *dillybag* (AustE): bag for carrying things of everyday use **75** *Yirrkala:* town in Arnhem Land, Northern Territory (cf. the map, inside cover) • *gouge sth.:* cut or scoop out sth. (here, a wooden surface) with a chisel (= Meisel) **84–85** *on a wholesale basis:* im Großhandel **90** *Alice Springs:* town in Australia's Northern Territory (cf. the map, inside cover) **93** *fabric* ['fæbrɪk]: Stoff **103** *custodian* (fml): person who takes responsibility for taking care of or protecting sth.

1. According to the text, what is the basis of all Aboriginal art (cf. ll. 6–21)?
2. Describe how the Walpiri-Pintubi communities of the western desert region use symbols in their 'ground designs' (l. 28).
3. According to the text, how does Aboriginal art find its way to the general public?
4. The text states that 'symbols and signs continue to be part of traditional Aboriginal communication' (ll. 68–69). Compare this with the role of symbols and signs as a form of communication in modern Western society. Use examples where possible.
5. Find examples of Aboriginal art in addition to the ones found in this book. Working in pairs or groups, discuss and make a list of visual characteristics (symbols, colours, techniques, etc.) which these artworks have in common. Compare and discuss your results with the other groups.
6. What aspects of the Aboriginal art which you have seen do you personally find attractive or interesting? Explain your answer.

Acknowledgements

Texts **I/1** From *Encyclopedia Australia* (Webster Publishing, Sydney, 1996). **I/2** From 'Waltzing the Outback' by Geoffrey Blainey, *The Age*, May 23, 1998. Reprinted by permission. **I/3** From *Mutant Message Down Under* by Marlo Morgan (Harper Collins, London, 1995). Reprinted by permission. **I/4** 'Australia' by A. D. Hope, Courtesy Curtis Brown (Aust) Pty Ltd, Sydney. **I/5** From 'On Having Half a Ball' by Ross Campbell, *Reader's Digest*, 1971. **II/1** From *Songs of the Dreamtime* by Terry Gandadila (Fidado Pty Ltd, Perth, 1995). Reprinted by permission of Terry Gandadila (for Jack Wunuwun). **II/2** From 'In Your Face Culture' by Kerry-Anne Walsh, *The Bulletin*, August 30, 1994. Reprinted by permission. **II/3** From 'Thrice, a Cry for Freedom and a Better Life', *The Age*, June 11, 2000. Reprinted by permission. **II/4** 'Living on the Edge' by Sally Heath and Mark Baker, *The Age*, March 22, 1998. Reprinted by permission. **II/5** From *The Custodians* by Nichola Jose (Picador, Sydney 1998). Reprinted by permission of Cameron Creswell Agency, Sydney. **III/1** From 'Making Tracks', *The Australian*, November 23–24, 1996. Reprinted by permission. **III/2** From *Remembering Babylon* by David Malouf (Chatto & Windus, London, 1994). Reprinted by permission. **III/3** From *Frontier* by Henry Reynolds (Allen & Unwin Pty Ltd, Sydney, 1987). Reprinted by permission. **III/4** 'One Hundred and Fifty Years' by Jack Davis, Courtesy Curtis Brown (Aust) Pty Ltd, Sydney. **III/5** From *The Custodians* by Nicholas Jose (Picador, Sydney, 1998). Reprinted by permission of Cameron Creswell Agency, Sydney. **III/6** From 'The Real Australia' by Robert Hughes, *Time*, September 25, 2000. Reprinted by permission. **IV/1** 'Backyard' by John Tranter, Courtesy Curtis Brown (Aust) Pty Ltd, Sydney. **IV/2** From 'Just Doin' It' by Sophie Tedmanson, *The Australian*, January 3–4, 1998. Reprinted by permission. **IV/3** From 'Olympics Gave Indigenous Australians Their Biggest Ever Stage' by Mike Corder, *The Independent*, October 2, 2000. Reprinted with permission of The Associated Press. **IV/4** From *The Age*, June 7, 1998. Reprinted by permission. **IV/5** From *Boomerang* by George Mikes (Andre Deutsch, London, 1968). Reprinted by permission of Judy Evans (Judy Mikes). **IV/6** From *The Cambridge Encyclopedia of Australia* by Susan Bambrick (Cambridge University Press, 1994). Reprinted by permission.

Illustrations Action Press, Hamburg: pp. 7 (© Dieter Kreuzkamp), 79 (© Mike Powell/Allsport Photograph); The Age, Melbourne: pp. 33 (© Bryan Charlton), 35 (© Craig Sillitoe), 38–40 (© Palani Mohan), 71 (right, © Angela Wylie); Archiv für Kunst und Geschichte, Berlin: pp. 15, 42 (© Henning Bock), 48; Australian Tourist Commission, Frankfurt/Main: cover (top right), pp. 10–11 (street sign); Dr. Volkhard Binder, Berlin: inside cover; Corel Library: p. 11 (Canberra); Deutsche Presse-Agentur, Frankfurt/Main: pp. 19 (bottom, © Torsten Blackwood), 60 (© Greg Wood), 68–69 (© Olivier Morin); Mary Evans Picture Library, London: p. 19 (top); Focus, Hamburg: p. 13 (man, ©Stéphan Korb); Getty Images/Bavaria, Munich: pp. 11 (sheep), 16–17, 45–47 (backdrop); Getty Images/Stone, Munich: pp. 11 (top, © Mark Segal), 11 (bottom right, © Paul Chesley), 43 (Ayers Rock, © Robert van der Hilst), 63 (barbecue, © John Lamb), 63–64 (bottom, © Kelvin Murray), 66 (girls © Carlos Serrao), 66–67 (boy, © Stuart McClymont); Gabriele Heinisch, Berlin: p. 23; The Holmes à Court Collection, Heytesbury: pp. 25, 26 (top), 26 (bottom), 27; Rudi Hurzlmeier, Munich: p. 21; Impact Photos, London: p. 36 (© Neil Morrison); National Library of Australia, Canberra: p. 18 (top); Panos Pictures, London: pp. 54 (young initiate, © Alastair McNaughton), 54 (top right, © John Miles), 57–59 (© Alastair McNaughton); Picture Press, Hamburg: cover (bottom, © Christine Osborne/Corbis), cover (middle left, © Bill Varie/Corbis), pp. 8 (left, © David Samuel Robbins/Corbis), 8 (middle, © Christine Osborne/Corbis), 8 (right, © Catherine Karnow/Corbis), 12–13 (© Penny Tweedie/Corbis), 19 (soldier, © Hulton-Deutsch Collection), 28 (© Paul A. Souders/Corbis), 32 (© Howard Davies/Corbis), 33 (left, © Howard Davies/Corbis), 43 (bottom, © Catherine Karnow/Corbis), 45 (top, © E. O Hoppé/Corbis), 53 (top, © Matthew McKee/Eye Ubiquitous), 53 (bottom, © Matthew McKee/Eye Ubiquitous), 63 (top right, © Bob Rowan/Corbis), 65 (© Robert Garvey/Corbis), 71 (© Owen Franken/Corbis); Reuters News Pictures, Berlin: p. 61 (© Mark Baker); Royal Flying Doctor Service of Australia, Sydney: p. 9; State Library of New South Wales, Sydney: pp. 5 (Image Library), 31 (Mitchell Library), 52 (Image Library); Wildlight Photo Agency, Sydney: cover (top, © David Moore), pp. 73 (man, © Grenville Turner), 73 (woman, © Jason Busch), 76 (middle, left © Carolyn Johns), 77 (bottom right, © Grenville Turner), 76–79 (© Grenville Turner); zefa visual media, Hamburg: p. 13 (woman, © Austen).